Contents

James O'Halloran SDB

Small Christian Communities

A PASTORAL COMPANION

 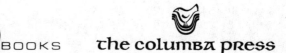

First published in 1996 by

Ireland:
THE COLUMBA PRESS
93 The Rise, Mount Merrion, Blackrock, Co Dublin
ISBN 1 85607 147 2

USA:
ORBIS BOOKS
Maryknoll, N.Y. 10545
ISBN 1-57075-077-7
Cataloging-in-Publication data available from the Library of Congress

Cover by Bill Bolger
The emblem on the cover is the logo of the European Network of Small Christian Communities and is used by kind permission.
Origination by The Columba Press
Printed in Ireland by Colour Books Ltd, Dublin
Copyright © 1996, James O'Halloran SDB

Introduction

I can think of no better way to introduce this book than to recall the story with which I began *Signs of Hope*. A tourist was travelling through rural Ireland and wasn't quite sure of his bearings. He therefore asked a farmer, working in a nearby field, if he were on the correct road to Askeaton. Wishing to be as courteous and sensitive as possible to the predicament of the tourist, the farmer replied, 'Well, you're on the right road to Askeaton all right. It's just that you're facin' in the wrong direction.'

This volume is not intended as a handbook. However, I hope it provides some suggestions and guidelines, or signposts, that may at least keep people who are developing small Christian communities facing in the right general direction. Then, by walking, they can forge a path, as a Spanish proverb puts it. The work builds on the original *Living Cells*, which was described by the *Tablet* as 'one of the best introductions to small Christian communities' and by the *National Catholic Reporter* as 'clear about the elements of a viable ecclesial community for the … 21st century.' It is the product of my being part of the small Christian community experience worldwide for twenty-five years (with a predilection for Africa and Latin America) as member, resource person, and animator. As well as the two areas mentioned, I have also had the good fortune of working in England, Ireland, Scotland, Malta, the United States, Canada, Australia, and Thailand. The book, in short, is offered as a pastoral companion; let it be your servant, not your master. Diversity and flexibility are affirmed in its pages.

As previous works did, this one also strives to deal with the theory and practice of small Christian communities, yet several new features appear. The following are some of them:

- a reordering and enhancement of the subject matter to make the volume even more user-friendly,

- a fuller and more effective use of the word of God,
- a complete historical profile of small Christian communities in the world,
- a sensitivity to the ecumenical and feminist dimensions,
- input of a psychological and sociological nature (leadership skills; conflict resolution etc.),
- a doubling of the examples that float possibilities for meetings,
- a methodology for pastoral planning honed by further experience,
- a chapter on the burning issues that arise in groups,
- a chapter on contemplation in the small communities,
- and another on their spirituality, drawn from the faith experiences of existing groups,
- an augmented list of passages for Bible sharing, arranged under relevant headings,
- an updated and annotated bibliography which must include nearly every significant book written in English on the subject of small Christian communities, and which also contains the details on invaluable resource books of all kinds for the lives and meetings of the communities,
- notes and index,
- and frequent stories and illustrations taken from *the lives of real groups* that hopefully make this book an interesting read.

Instead of using the he/she form, for the most part I try to vary the personal pronoun from one part of the book to another.

I should like to thank all those members of small Christian communities who shared with me over the past twenty-five years. This is their book. For there aren't any experts on the groups; only little people with little experiences to share. However, I take the liberty of mentioning some persons who contributed to this work in a more immediate way:

- the members of my own family,
- my religious community (I am a Salesian of Don Bosco),
- the members past and present of my own small Christian community in Crumlin, Dublin,
- the first groups with whom I worked in Quito, Ecuador,
- the small communities in St Martin's Parish in Freetown (Sierra Leone),

- Salvatore Colombo, Sean Devereaux, Felim McAllister, Sr Barbara, and the African catechist James – friends and martyrs for the kingdom,
- Monica Ballestrem, Tony Byrne CSSp, Jim and Ursula Cranswick, Ruth Egar RSM, Colleen Fleischmann, Ian and the late Margaret Fraser, Rolf Goldstein, Stephen Harris, James Kelly SJ, Alexio Manyanda, Jack McHugh CSSp, Don Mullan, Joe Murray, Frank Naughton CSSp, Sr Teresa Nyarambi, Proinsias Ó Donnchadha, Sile O'Reilly, Mario Paredes, Joseph Prased Pinto OFM Cap., Christian Smith, Max Stetter, and Paiboon Teepakorn,
- scripture scholars Michelle Connolly, David Efroymson, Bill Loader, and Elaine Wainwright (I learned much from working with them),
- The faculty of Graduate Religion at La Salle University, Philadelphia, and
- Misereor and Trócaire, who have encouraged and provided some financial backing for the project.

And, finally, thanks are due to Seán O Boyle, The Columba Press, and his staff; and to Bob Gormley, Robert Ellsberg, Sue Perry, and their team at Orbis Books.

PART I

Historical Profile

CHAPTER 1

A Historical Profile of Small Christian Communities

Until the 1960s a hierarchical model of Church prevailed in the world, but with Vatican II we entered a period of change. The Council called on the Church to be community as the Trinity is community (*Dogmatic Constitution of the Church, 4*). In the intervening years we have found that one effective way of realizing this vision is through small Christian communities, which then combine into larger units to form *a communion of communities*.

The appearance of the groups was not a bolt from the blue. Their history dates not merely from the 1950s and 60s; it reaches much further back. And all of it is important. In the various countries where I work, I find that those involved in the groups are most curious to learn about similar experiences elsewhere, and about the origins of the small communities in the first place. Which led to my elaborating this profile. Not that the ordinary people need all the details here recorded, yet having a general picture is most helpful.

This is so for a variety of reasons:
- When the folk in communities know that they are not alone in the world, it can be a *great support*.
- They get a sense of *the Holy Spirit at work everywhere*.
- And a sense of the *New Pentecost* ushered in by John XXIII.
- The power the groups have to *communicate Christ* and his good news also becomes obvious.
- And people are saved from having to *reinvent the wheel* or eternally repeat *the mistakes* of history.

Small Christian communities in the New Testament

'Who was the founder of the small Christian communities anyway? Was it you?' someone once asked me during a workshop on the subject.

'No,' I replied mightily relieved at not having to shoulder that Messianic burden.

'Who was it then?'

'Well, actually, it was Jesus Christ.'

In a sense the communities are as new as the shopping mall, yet as old as the gospel. They have their origins in the itinerant community that trod the dusty roads of Palestine with Jesus, in the gathering of the early Christians which formed in Jerusalem after the first Pentecost (cf. Acts 2: 42-47; 4: 32-37), and in all those groups that sprang up in the gentile world largely as a result of Paul's work.

If the reader would like to explore the life of those early Christian communities, there are a number of texts that would allow her to do so. Reflecting on them can tell us much about the joys and sorrows, sufferings and struggles of the early Christians. For the sake of convenience we list them here:

- *Jerusalem:* Luke 24:52-53; Acts 2:22-6:15; 7:54-8:4; 11:22; 11:27-30; 15:1-31; 21:7-20.
- *Antioch:* Acts 11:19-30; 13:1-3; 14:21-28; 15:1-35; Galatians 2:11.
- *Ephesus:* Acts 18:19-28; 19:1-41; 20:16-38; Ephesians 1:1-12; 6:21-24; 1 Corinthians 15:32; 16:8; 1 Timothy 1:3-4; Revelation 2:1-7.
- *Philippi:* Acts 16:11-24; Philippians 1:3-14; 2:25-30; 4:14-23; Thessalonians 2:2.
- *Corinth:* Acts 18:1-11; 19:1; 1 Corinthians 1:10-31; 3:3-9; 3:16-23; 4:17-21; 5:1-2; 6:5-11; 8:4-13; 9:1-7; 9:11-16; 10:14-22; 11:17-34; 12:4-31; 13:1-13; 14:1-33; 15:3-19; 16:10-12; 16:13-20; 2 Corinthians 1:12-24; 2:4.

There are those who believe that Christ left us a highly organized Church, rather along the lines that we have experienced until modern times. Many scripture scholars would not agree. Raymond Brown, for example, has pointed out that even in New Testament times the Church expressed itself in diverse forms.[1] They were as follows:

- The heritage that Paul leaves us in the pastoral epistles of Titus and 1 and 2 Timothy. This model *emphasizes Church organization.* Authority is important, because the times are precarious, and, consequently, the role of presbyter-bishop is stressed. It proposes *a family* approach.
- Then there is the type that considers the Church as *Christ's body*

to be loved which can be found in Colossians and Ephesians, and is also traced to Paul.

- From the Gospel of Luke and the Acts we get a third Pauline mode, namely, *the Church and the Spirit*. This highlights the presence and action of the Spirit.
- In 1 Peter we find the Petrine heritage of the Church seen as *people of God*, a form that makes a person feel a strong sense of belonging.
- There is the tradition of John in the Fourth Gospel which shows people as *a community of disciples personally attached to Jesus*.
- John provides a further model in his epistles: *a community of persons guided by the Paraclete-Spirit*.
- And, finally, there is the heritage of Jewish-Gentile Christians in the Gospel of Matthew, which stresses *'an authority that doesn't stifle Jesus.'*

In the foregoing models the Church as *community*, or *people of God*, is strongly represented. Where authority is emphasized it is never intended to be dominating, rather is it to be understood as *service*. As Hoornaert points out: 'Nothing could have been further from the spirit of primitive Christianity than the notion of a power or authority that would not be one of sisterly or brotherly service. The principle of a community of brothers and sisters forbade any arrogance of power and held up before the eyes of all the example of Christ:

Though he was in the form of God,
he did not deem equality with God
something to be grasped at.
Rather he emptied himself
and took on the form of a slave ... (Philippians 2: 6-7).[2]

It would be quite mistaken then to look back and read the history of the early Christians with spectacles tinted by our own times.

Paul's approach

For Paul, the Church is the body of Christ (cf. 1 Corinthians 12:27) and as such clearly a *community*. No doubt the words spoken by the Lord on the road to Damascus had branded themselves into his consciousness: 'Saul, Saul why do you persecute *me*?' (Acts 9:4). Paul would understand community, or *being together in Christ*, as:

- living as a single, united body, where the Spirit of God brings forth the fruits of the Spirit (cf. Galatians 5:16-25).
- being able to discern matters for itself with the help of the Spirit (cf. 1 Corinthians 2: 6-16; 4: 6-7; 6: 1-8; 7: 10-12; 12:4-11).
- being responsible, or:
  - faithful to its call (cf. Galatians 3:1-5; 5:1; 5:13-15),
  - capable of drawing others to Christ (1 Thessalonians 4:9-12),
  - being ready to get involved with the groaning of *all* creation (Romans 8:18-25),
- struggling with various issues, such as:
  - the fact that the kingdom of God is already existing, yet will only be fully realized in the world to come (cf. 1 Corinthians 15: 12-28);
  - the delay in Jesus' Second Coming, or the Parousia (cf. 1 Thessalonians 5:1-11; 2 Thessalonians 2:1-12);
  - anxiety over death (cf. 1 Thessalonians 4:13-18; 1 Corinthians 15:12-28);
  - morality and a false sense of security (cf. 1 Corinthians 3:18-23; 5:1-2; 5:8; 6:12-20; 8:1-13; 10:23-11:1; Romans 14:13-23; 15:1-6);
  - and the conflict between Jewish and Gentile Christians (cf. Galatians 2:1-3:14).[3]

In the Pauline communities, as indeed in all the early Christian groups, it is *people* who are important. Organization and buildings are secondary. The faithful meet in homes; there are no churches. So in Acts 12:12 we read of their being gathered in the house of John Mark when Peter comes knocking at the door, and in Romans 16:5 Paul sends greetings to the Church that meets in the house of Priscilla and Aquila (cf. also Romans 16:11 and 16:14-15). A significant fact emerges here; Christians met in homes and it was there that they got the experience of the *intimate group*.

But there was also the preoccupation of bringing the small communities together on occasions so as to get the equally important experience of being *a communion of communities*. The Temple in Jerusalem was an early meeting point. And at Antioch later the Acts tell us of all the people being gathered together in one place by Paul and Barnabas, when they returned from what is known as Paul's first missionary journey (cf. 14:26-27).

Of course the communitarian thrust of the Church was inspired

by the example of Jesus. He formed a community of disciples, consisting of men and women, around himself, and as part of that community set about the task of preaching the good news. While growing up, he would have been aware of the many groups that were
common in the Roman world: Scribes, Pharisees, Saducees, Essenes,
Epicureans, Stoics, Cynics, and so forth. Each sabbath he frequented
the synagogue.

Nazareth was situated on a great trading route. All manner of
people would have passed that way, including Jews from every
part of the Roman Empire on their way to worship in Jerusalem.
Furthermore, Nazareth was only five kilometres from Sepphoris
which was rebuilt during the youth of Jesus as a Hellenistic, or cult-
urally Greek, city. Capernaum, where he later lived, was a northern
border town to the Decapolis region of ten Hellenistic cities. So
Christ grew up in a Galilee that we could almost describe as multi-
cultural.[4] He must have come across wandering philosophers and
gurus holding forth in the marketplace and undoubtedly learned
from all his experiences (cf. Luke 2:52). One of the lessons that he
must have absorbed was the effectiveness of the group. It is not surprising then that we find him adopting the strategy of the small
community in his own ministry.

Sometimes there is the perception that all was light and sweetness in the early Christian groups. By no means. And if we think
our times are difficult, theirs were still more so. As we saw above,
the fledgling Church had to deal with a host of troubles. But the
remarkable, and seemingly contradictory, thing was that *their unity
was forged from the very struggle and suffering which they endured in
common.* This, surely, should be a source of encouragement for us in
dealing with confrontation and conflict today.

Change with Constantine

With the coming of the Roman Emporer Constantine (288-337 C.E.)
the Church changed from a communitarian model to a hierarchical
one. Though he was principally responsible for the change, it is
only fair to say that small compromises can be detected even in The
New Testament. Thus in 1 Peter 2:18 we read: 'Servants be submis-
sive to your masters with all respect, not only to the kind and gentle
but also to the overbearing.' Here we see the Church adapting to

survive; the old patriarchal, or dominating, order is reasserting itself. Be good servants and you will be considered as having worth is the message. A modification of the gospel, where our worth comes from being human persons, children of God, and brothers and sisters in Christ. But at the particular time these words were written, patriarchy was being strongly affirmed right across the Roman Empire.

The seachange, however, came with the conversion of Constantine. The Church ceased to be harassed and Christianity became the favoured religion of the Empire. It was fashionable to be a Christian and the Church greatly increased in numbers. Yet it lost the momentum of an entity that until then had been lean, persecuted, and more committed; the edge of witness became blunted. In the mid-fourth century bishops were installed as public officials. This gave birth to a Church model that was both hierarchical and strongly institutional, a form that prevailed as the communitarian vision faded. The neighbour-hood community, or house Church (*oikos*), ceased to exist and the focus was placed on structures. With the departure of the house Church, a dimension that gave early Christianity much of its vitality was gone. And, truth to tell, the Church has never been quite the same without it. Today the ordinary faithful are reclaiming their heritage as small communities increase in numbers around the world. That Christians enjoy this heritage is not simply an optional extra. It is *a right*; it is *a necessity*. I hope these things will become clear as the book proceeds.

Though the vision of Church as community faded, it was never entirely lost. It was preserved in a rarified fashion by the religious orders. We owe a debt of gratitude to figures like Basil, Benedict, Scholastica, Dominic, Francis, Clare, Ignatius, Teresa, John Bosco, and Mary of Mornese. The founders of religious orders and congregations were often charismatic figures who valued relationships above structures. Francis really lamented as Brother Elias boxed in his creativity, and Don Bosco was deeply distressed the day he saw his pupils being marshalled into lines to enter the classrooms. This had not been the practice and was not the *family spirit* that prevailed in the early days of his Oratory. In short the religious orders that appeared on the scene like a breath of fresh air often adapted to the pyramidal Church model, becoming little pyramids within the great pyramid. Nevertheless the founders must be credited with preserving a precious Christian memory.

Modern times

As already mentioned, small Christian communities are once again emerging among the baptized in our days. And it is happening worldwide.

Latin America

The Latin American communities began in Brazil, 1956. Leonardo Boff traces their beginnings to the lament of a humble old lady, so her words may be among the most momentous uttered in Church history. 'Christmas Eve,' she complained, 'all three Protestant churches were lit up and full of people ... And the Catholic Church closed and dark! ... Because we can't get a priest.'[5] The question naturally arose as to why everything should come to a standstill simply because there was no priest. This led to an initiative by Dom Agnello Rossi, prelate of Rio de Janeiro at the time, to launch a community catechetical movement in Barra do Parai, out of which small communities eventually emerged.

From Brazil they spread to Chile, Honduras, Panama, and with time to all Latin America. Estimates state that there are now between 180,000 and 200,000 groups in the sub-continent.[6] This growth was greatly encouraged by the meetings of the Latin American bishops at Medellin, Columbia, 1968; at Puebla, Mexico, 1979; and even at Santo Domingo, 1992, where the tone was much more traditional than in the previous meetings.

The main preoccupations of the communities in Latin America have been *justice and peace, the option with the poor,* and *the option with youth.* Indeed they have awakened the whole world to the importance of these items, largely through the foregoing sessions. In recent years *women's issues and the cause of the indigenous peoples* have forced their way on to the agenda. In terms of political involvement, the Church seems to be concentrating on furthering the *option with the poor* within the newly-forming democracies.

During the pontificate of Pope John Paul II there have been tensions between Rome and the Latin American Church. There was the conflict over Liberation Theology, heartache regarding the appointment of bishops who were regarded as overly conservative, and so on. These tensions naturally made life difficult for the small communities; some of the new appointees did not favour the groups. The options of Medellin and Puebla are still very much alive, however, because few bishops can remain indifferent to the utter misery of the overwhelming majority of their people, and many of the pastoral commissions operating at lower levels are forward-looking in their strategies. The small Christian communities, also, quietly carry on their work down among God's poor. This was borne out by a meeting of groups in São Paulo in 1995 where there was a ferment of ideas and a release of much energy and hope. An important national gathering of Brazilian small Christian communities, which is expected to chart their course for some years to come, is scheduled for 1997.

There have also been the challenges for the communities from without the Catholic Church in the form of the Protestant sects whose numbers are escalating dramatically. One such sect in Brazil has in fact grown from nine thousand members to three-and-a-half million within a relatively short period. Although the impact of these sects has some positive aspects, as we shall see later, I still feel that they are out of touch with many of the real problems of life. If the human person had only a soul to save and not a stomach to fill, they might prove more understandable.

During the oppressive military dictatorships of the 1970s, the small Christian communities alone provided a forum for dissident voices and the Church wielded great influence. Nowadays there are many avenues to protest and action: workers' parties, trade unions, students' movements, and so on. The role of the Church must now surely be to support all initiatives that strive to build a world that is more just, and attend pastorally to the hurt of people who are marginalized, or worse still, totally excluded by a heartless free-market system.

Finally, where the small communities are concerned, the prophetic process has now reached the stage where the groups feel the need for an organization that will be officially recognised – an organization, however, that will be at the service of people and have due regard for the autonomy of the communities.

North America (U.S.A. and Canada)

Small Christian communities are to be found in many denominations throughout the United States. There are English and Spanish-speaking groups.

The English-speaking communities would describe themselves as largely middle class and would critique themselves as tending to be inward looking, though the issue of solidarity with the poor is now being raised and action taken in quite effective ways. Michael Cowan[7] speaks of coalitions of small faith community networks which link with a variety of community organizations committed to transforming society. These are creating a base for change among ordinary citizens no matter what their race or creed, and many believe that they are altering the ways in which political and economic business is done. The Industrial Areas Foundation that flourishes in settings from Brooklyn to San Antonio to Los Angeles would be an example of this cooperation.

The situation even with regard to the small communities is affected by the individualism that is so deeply ingrained in the American psyche. The spirit of the ruggedly independent frontiersperson, a type of John Wayne syndrome, is still very much alive. In this respect there is another memory that needs recovering; it is the tradition of community that was an integral part of life among the early Puritan settlers under John Winthrop in seventeenth century New England.

There are small communities in Canada. I have encountered them in Ontario and Quebec and they exist in Alberta, British Columbia, Manitoba, and probably in other provinces as well. The groups share many of the problems of the United States. They too have to cope with people of different origins and cultures, mostly English and French, with the corresponding languages. But as in the United States, there are the native Indian cultures as well. In both countries the issue is the same: how to recognize and cherish varying cultures while at the same time integrating them into a harmonious whole. It admits of no easy solution. Though the Canadians have much in common with the United States, the problems are nevertheless profoundly flavoured by local history and circumstance.

The National Small Christian Community Convocation held at St Paul, Minnesota, 1993, was a significant gathering for the communities in North America. The *National Catholic Reporter* of August 27th that year had the following to say:

Almost all the 425 convocation participants, from 33 US states, five Canadian provinces and Australia, were white and middle class. Notably absent [Fr Bernard] Lee said, was any significant representation from 400 Hispanic small Christian communities, from communities connected with religious orders rather than parishes, and from 'free-floating' communities.

Nevertheless the gathering at the University of St Thomas was a landmark: the three groups representing US Christian communities at the diocesan, parish, and group level were meeting together for the first time on their own initiative. These groups are Buena Vista, the association of community members; the National Alliance of Parishes Restructuring into Communities, an association of parishes; and the North American Forum for Small Christian Communities an organization of diocesan personnel.[8]

Another group, Communitas in Washington D.C., which considers itself an intentional Eucharistic community that is not part of the Church structure, was not present on this occasion. The article does not mention yet another coordinating group, namely, Sojourners Outreach, Faith Communities for Justice, also based in Washington D. C.

The participants at the convocation exchanged experiences. They noted their origins in movements such as RENEW, RCIA, Cursillo, and Marriage Encounter. With Robert Pelton of Notre Dame and Barbara Howard, co-founder with her husband Michael of Buena Vista, many felt 'the major movement was in parishes.' Bernard Lee stressed the need to be in mission. 'I fear that because we are so middle class we might not take the social agenda seriously,' he said.

In terms of institutes Notre Dame University, Indiana; Loyola University in New Orleans; the Maryknoll School of Theology, New York; and MACC, the Mexican American Cultural Centre, in San Antonio, Texas, have, among others, shown an interest in small Christian communities. This interest has been backed up by a steady flow of literature on small communities and related areas from various sources, particularly from Orbis Books.

In their struggle with cultural problems, the small Christian communities in the United States and Canada will surely have much to say to the rest of the world. This is particularly the case in these days when ethnic strife and ethnic cleansing have reared their ugly heads in former Yugoslavia and Rwanda, and the peace processes in Northern Ireland and the Middle East are so delicately poised. They also have to cope with a harsh materialism that makes their task by no means easy, and their efforts to do so are an inspiration to all.

And the Spanish-speaking communities? On July 14, 1995, the *National Catholic Reporter* had this to say:

Fifty years after evangelization to Hispanics became a formal programme of the US Catholic Church, approximately 450 ministry leaders reaffirmed that commitment in San Antonio at a spirited convocation June 23-25.

The participants looked back over half a century of endeavour, noting the importance of the approval of the National Pastoral Plan for Hispanic Ministry in 1987 which called for:

- *small ecclesial communities,*
- parish renewal,
- youth ministry,
- promotion of family life, and
- leadership formation adapted to the Hispanic culture.

The plan in fact grew out of the US bishops' 1983 pastoral on *The Hispanic Presence: Challenge and Commitment;* national meetings of Hispanic Catholics held in 1972, 1977, and 1985 also helped the process.

The Convocation '95 produced a *Declaration of Commitment* which paid tribute to to the leading role that Hispanics had played in fighting for the family as the fundamental unit of society and the Church.

The document also urged those working in the Hispanic ministry to:

- Recognise the rights and dignity of the vocation of parents and of the rights of women in all aspects of social and religious life.
- Uphold the preferential option for (*sic*) the poor as an essential part of the Catholic faith.
- Affirm the dignity of human beings from the moment of conception until natural death.
- Recognize the right to dignified work, a just salary, decent housing, education that respects cultural differences, and access to decent health care.
- Affirm solidarity with farm workers, refugees, victims of politi-

cal abuse, and undocumented immigrants, with special attention given to discrimination against immigrants.[9]

Hispanic small Christian communities existed in the United States at least since the seventies in areas such as California, Florida, New Mexico, and Texas. In general, as in Latin America, justice has been a key preoccupation of the groups. There is the endeavour to link up with CELAM, the Latin American Bishops' Conference, and this no doubt is also with a view to preparing for the First Pan American Synod, which John Paul II has scheduled for the end of the century.

Africa

During the 1971 Synod of Bishops in Rome, the Africans present noted that small Christian communities already existed in Africa. And this quite independently of what had happened in Latin America. One cannot say for certain where the modern groups began. *They sprang up spontaneously throughout the world at roughly the same historical period by the power of the Holy Spirit.*

When I first started to work with African communities in 1980, I noted two things that were often lacking. The first was that the members were not clear on the vision, or theology, that accompanied the communities, and then there was no great urgency in the matter of justice. There was the mistaken notion that where you had a small number of people, there you had a small Christian community. Even among a reduced group of people you can of course find those who dominate, and this is definitely not community. Or some divided a parish up into zones as if the concept was about territory rather than people. Needless to say, the vision has been clarified during the intervening years.

In 1980 most African countries had been independent for a relatively short period and for the first time in recent history had their own governments. People were happy with this new-found freedom and not overly critical. However, with the passing years they have realized that not only colonizers oppress, but also your own politicians when corrupt. Meanwhile the Church has spoken out and acted in the cause of justice. Nelson Mandela in fact thanked the Churches for the role they played in overcoming apartheid; South Africa had of course been politicized for decades on this issue. The Kenyan bishops too have since been most valiant in opposing oppression in their country, and we could give many more instances. Nor are prophetic documents wanting. The following are examples: *Seeking Gospel Justice in Africa,*[10] *Centenary of the Evangelization in Kenya,*[11] and *The African Synod.*[12]

The small Christian communities have also stood up on justice issues. According to animators in the field, the groups in Zambia played 'a considerable role' in that country's peaceful transition from one-party state to multi-party democracy. In Kenya too during the 1993 elections the ordinary community members surprised politicians by speaking out on what they felt was for the good of the country. In the past those politicians had been accustomed to dealing with the people through intermediaries such as pastors. One member of parliament even asked pointedly whether *Father* were not present. The people answered no, but that they themselves would discuss the relevant issues.

The following proved encouraging landmarks for the promotion of small Christian communities in Africa, making it clear that they were *a priority* on the continent:

- the Fifth AMECEA (Association of Member Episcopal Conferences of Eastern Africa) Plenary Conference in Nairobi, 1973,
- Sixth AMECEA Plenary Conference at Nairobi, 1976,
- Seventh AMECEA Plenary Conference at Zomba, Malawi, 1979,
- the Apostolic Visit to Kenya by Pope John Paul II, 1980,
- The SECAM (Symposium of Episcopal Conferences in Africa and Madagascar) Assemblies at Yaounde, Cameroons, 1981, and Kinshasa, Zaire, 1984,
- the First Plenary session of IMBISA (Inter-Regional Meeting of Bishops of Southern Africa), Chishawasha, Zimbabwe, 1984,
- the pastoral letter of the Kenyan Catholic bishops entitled *Centenary of the Evangelization in Kenya,* 1989,
- the Eleventh Assembly of the AMECEA bishops, Lusaka, Zambia, 1992 ('Small Christian communities are no longer merely an option,' the meeting declared; an expression of conviction rather than a pulling of rank),
- The African Synod of Bishops, Rome, 1994, where the notion of *Family Church* emerged and, consequently, the communities received wide support (Bishop Jodo Siloto of Mozambique, for example, '... saw these communities as an expression of African

communitarianism, and the only true way of inculturation for the African Church. In fact, he said, any pastoral strategy that omitted small Christian communities would be creating a Church without a future.'),[13]

- then there was the visit of Pope John Paul II to the Cameroons, Kenya, and South Africa in September 1995 to launch the document *Ecclesia in Africa* (*The Church in Africa*) which resulted from the Synod of the previous year. In no 63 of this Post-Synodal Exhortation the Holy Father reiterated the resolve of the gathering to implement Family Church.

I have heard a number of African bishops express sentiments similar to those of Bishop Jodo Siloto above. We can understand what they are saying if we consider the realities of their situation: immense difficulties of transportation and communication, areas of open hostility, volatile political scenes, famine, refugees, the precarious position of missionaries and even of local priests and religious, an acute shortage of vocations to the priesthood and religious life. What can be done in the face of all this but dot the landscape with small communities that are autonomous, yet linked through the communion of communities? The words of Irenaeus are relevant here: 'Where there are three people, there is the Church. Laity will suffice.' And he was not being patronizing. After all, through baptism we all become part of a priestly people and even ministerial priests would not make much sense outside of this context. To whom would they minister?

By training animators, pastoral centres have done much to promote the groups throughout Africa. Kenema in Sierra Leone, Gaba in Kenya, and Lumko in South Africa would be instances of this. But nowadays many dioceses have their own pastoral centres which also do sterling work in the field.

At a conservative estimate there are reckoned to be 10,000 small Christian communities in East Africa.[14] It is true that some of them would be prayer groups at the moment rather than communities, yet they are moving in the direction of becoming Family Church. Before the troubles there were an estimated 300 cells in Sierra Leone, and in South Africa 70% of the parishes are working towards their establishment either directly or through the RENEW programme. On a recent visit to Zimbabwe I was told in one diocese that they had 600 groupings. Unfortunately there are no exact statistics for the continent; hence the sporadic nature of the foregoing. However, one can safely say that there are thousands and thousands of small communities and that their number continues to grow.

An interesting feature of the African small Christian communities is that they are well integrated into the mainstream Church. It is true that the original inspiration came from the bishops rather than the grassroots, and some would consider this a weakness. However, we all belong to the Family Church and, such being the case, does it really matter where the inspiration comes from? The question is whether or not the people make it their own. My own experience leads me to answer with a resounding yes to this question. Indeed I feel that it was a pity that our missionaries did not go to Africa with a communitarian model of Church in the first instance, because traditionally there was a great sense of family and community there even before we arrived. Indeed their strong sense of family and community is the special gift of the African groups to the rest of the world. That communal instinct is under intense pressure nowadays both from within and without the continent; from without there comes an ethos of individualism and economic exploitation, from within the ills just mentioned above. Nevertheless the family and the community are still holding fast.

Generally speaking the communities throughout the world have remained within the mainstream Churches. Some are situated at the heart of these Churches, as in Africa, others in the margins. Many feel that the life is to be found in the margins and it is there we must look for renewal. There is the fear that, if the groups are mainstream, they can be absorbed into the institution and manipulated. I doubt it. I have seen many places where the communities are now thriving, yet initially they were warily received by the clergy. The decisive factor was the enthusiasm of the laity. We are entering upon the age of the laity and it is they who will largely shape the Church of the future. As already noted, priests are in short supply. 'After all,' I once heard an African bishop say, 'Many of our people are lucky if they see a priest once a year.' Furthermore not only are the small communities manifestations of a fresh communitarian mode of Church, they can also be powerful instruments for creating it. Once the members take the Bible in their hands, reflect on the word of God, and take responsibility to act upon it, things can never be quite the same again.

So who is to say whether salvation is in the margins or the mainstream? I don't think we can confine the Holy Spirit to the one or the other. Very likely renewal will come in a variety of ways.

Finally, the African groups are not without their problems. These are the main issues that preoccupy them:

- the difficulty of involving men,
- how to integrate youth,
- how women are to play their full part,
- problems in finding appropriate leaders,
- wrangles over money,
- what to do about non-sacramental Christians (normally there is a great openness towards them),
- deciding a suitable agenda for meetings,
- and a whole plethora of issues surrounding culture (e.g. tribal divisions, superstition, and so forth).

We shall touch on many of these problems in the course of this volume, particularly in chapter 5. The efforts at resolving them should be most enlightening for communities the world over.

Asia

When we think of Asia, what comes to mind is the geographical vastness of the continent and the enormous variety of cultures, languages, social and economic conditions, and indeed religions. Where religions are concerned, Asia boasts a rich heritage with roots in Hinduism, Buddhism, Islam, Sinhala, Shintoism, and Confucianism. These can have their own sophisticated thought-systems and some are older than Christianity. Then there are also vital popular and local expressions of these faiths. From these religions there have been reactions to Christ that cross a wide spectrum from total rejection as a colonial intruder to complete acceptance as Saviour of the world. Before saying a word about small Christian communities in Asia, therefore, I feel that I should pay respects to all this richness and complexity; it must always be borne in mind.

However, having said this, small Christian communities do exist in China, East Timor (currently occupied by Indonesia), Hong Kong, India, Indonesia, Japan, Laos, Pakistan, the Philippines, and Sri Lanka. Hong Kong is to rejoin China in 1997 and just now this has led to a great surge of interest in the small communities there, as a strategy for survival in difficult situations.

Small Christian communities, as such, would be most numerous in the Philippines which is in fact one of the great growth areas for the groups in the world. As in Latin America, the issues are poverty, oppression, cultural alienation, sexual exploitation, environmental abuse, and a crying need for land reform. In the Philippines, also, they are elaborating an appropriate theology for their situation, not a theology of liberation, but a theology of struggle, accompanied by a Good Friday spirituality of the cross. Until now we have focused a lot on the experience of the groups in Latin America, but the story of the Philippines is one waiting to be fully told. And we would all undoubtedly benefit from the telling. One of the significant factors in the proliferation of the communities throughout the land was the presence everywhere of committed and valiant religious sisters, some of whom did not hesitate to lie down before oncoming tanks to bring down the oppressive Marcos' regime.

The story of small Christian communities in China, as related by Raymond Fung,[15] is truly amazing. We thought that everything Christian was pretty well wiped out by the persecution of Mao. Not so. When he disappeared off the scene and the situation eased somewhat, house Churches, animated by lay people, surfaced in that great country – house Churches whose faith was all the deeper for the untold hardships they had endured for long, bitter years.

On thinking of Asia, India and Pakistan come very much into the frame. Pastoral workers there cite some formidable obstacles to the formation of small communities: a sense of belonging that doesn't extend beyond family and caste, the deeply ingrained caste and class basis of society, gender barriers, uncommitted Christians, and the fact that these Christians are often few in number and widely scattered. Jesus, of course, with his strong emphasis on communion offers the possibility of bridging these divides. Furthermore his vision of the kingdom of God extends this hope beyond the confines of family, ethnic group, and the Church itself to the whole of society. Indeed there has been some focus on inter-faith dialogue in the sub-continent with Hindus, Buddhists, Muslims, and others, though more undoubtedly needs to be done in this regard.

Justice is another area that is receiving attention in India and Pakistan; indeed it was highlighted as an important feature of an

African and Asian ethos at the Consultation on African and Asian Spirituality held in Colombo, 18-25 June, 1992. Hence there is actually a growing concern for the issue in the Churches all over Asia; the ethos and activism of the Christian Workers' Fellowship in Sri Lanka would be a good example of this. And Minjung Theology in Korea, which leads to protest and action from the oppressed against oppressive elites, whether civil or religious, would be another. The *minjung*, or aware people, as opposed to the *daejung*, or confused masses, are terms deeply rooted in Korean tradition.

In his book, *Inculturation Through Basic Communities*, Joseph Prased Pinto cites the sentiments of a seminar on small Christian communities held in Bangalore, 1981, which regretted that the Indian bishops did not show more interest in the emergence of the groups.[16] Prased Pinto informs me that this has now changed; virtually every bishop wants to facilitate small Christian communities in his diocese. Many dioceses have in fact introduced them. Foremost among them would be those of Bombay, Kottar, Tuticorin, Trivandrum, Alleppey, Mangalore, Pune, Patna, Guntur, and Hyderbad.

Frequent training programmes of a pastoral and animating nature are held in Bombay, Patna, Andhra, Bangalore, and other venues. Much useful material has been published at Secunderabad, NBCLC, Bangalore, St Paul's Allhabad, and elsewhere. Owing to the rich diversity of language (India has 16) and culture, mentioned above, there is a difficulty in coordinating programmes nationwide. There is, also, a dearth of scientific studies, though many seminarians have written useful dissertations.

Among many others, Bishop Bosco Penha of Bombay and Fr P. H. Edwin of Kottar have contributed much to the birth of small Christian communities in India.

When dealing with Africa above, we noted how the cause of the communities had been furthered by pastoral centres. In the continent under consideration, too, the East Asian Pastoral Centre in Manila has done much to propagate the idea.

Noting that the Church is essentially 'communion-koinonia, a people made one with the Father, the Son and Holy Spirit,'[17] the official Church has focused upon, and affirmed the concept of, small Christian communities at a number of key gatherings. The following are some of them:

- the Asian Colloquium on Ministries in the Church, Hong Kong, 1977,
- International Mission Congress, Manila, 1979,
- The Second Bishops' Institute for Missionary Apostolate of the Federation of Asian Bishops' Conferences, Ponmudi, Trivandrum, 1980 (limited to the countries of South Asia: Pakistan, Bangladesh, Sri Lanka, and India),
- a Bangalore Seminar on Basic Christian Communities, 1981,
- The Third Plenary Assembly of the Federation of Asian Bishops' Conferences, Samphran, 1982, and
- an Asian Synod, it would seem, is being mooted for the not-too-distant future.

Lastly, we look to Asia for inspiration in the areas of *contemplation and celebration*. Indeed many young people from the West go to India, for example, in search of *the holy*. There is, however, the growing awareness that to be authentic this contemplation must issue in action. And there is also a deep love of celebration in the Orient. In Japan, for instance, a great sense of festivity with its origins in Shintoism leads people to rejoice in the primal unity of the Trinity, the community of God. 'All comes from God and strives to return to God, until the Almighty becomes "all in all" (2 Corinthians 15:28). This faith gives the Christian a deep optimism.'[18]

Of course Japan is one of the most powerful industrial nations of the world and might be considered as having cause for celebration. What people in the North sometimes find strange is the presence of this spirit of celebration in impoverished countries. Perhaps they do not understand the great value of celebration as well as their less affluent brothers and sisters. I have found that Latin Americans and Africans celebrate with equal enthusiasm, whether the occasion be liturgical or social.

Australia and New Zealand

One finds small Christian communities all over Australia. Many of them would be 15 years on the road, though the origins of some would even go back to the fifties; for example there were the Newman Societies and Christian Life Movement among the Roman Catholics in Adelaide and Melbourne. And since the early seventies there have been the Protestant Independent House Churches in

Canberra. The vast majority of the present groups would be non-residential but frequently meet in homes or some other appropriate location. In addition there are a number of impressive residential communities such as Ain Karim (Bunbury), Exodus (Perth), St Joseph's House of Prayer (Goulburn), L'Arche (Canberra), the Gentle Bunyip (Melbourne).

Many Catholic dioceses have pastoral teams that are actively encouraging the formation of groups. I found this to be the case in Melbourne, Canberra, Brisbane, Rockhampton, Townsville, Adelaide, Perth, and Bunbury. The Canberra team was in fact ecumenical in its composition. The Archbishop of Adelaide, Leonard Faulkner, proclaimed a vision for the archdiocese in 1989 and entitled it *Vision for the World*. This called for a leadership in world affairs, supported by the formation of small Christian communities. In 1994 his pastoral letter, entitled *Community for the World*, encouraged the setting up of small Christian communities within the archdiocese. Bishop Benjamin of Townsville in Queensland has set forth a similar vision, called *The Townsville Experiment*, for the people of his diocese.

One of the pleasing things about Australia is that the communities are to be found right across the denominations. There is, therefore, the ecumenical dimension, though some would feel that Roman Catholics are lagging somewhat regarding ecumenism at the moment. Indeed Communities Australia, an ecumenical group in Melbourne, have done much, particularly through their magazine of the same name, to foster and link small communities. They also invited a number of resource persons from overseas to come and share experiences with the Australian Churches.

These Churches are singularly blessed in the quality of their lay leaders. Where Catholicism is concerned, these leaders seem to have come largely from the Young Christian Workers and Students of the forties, fifties and sixties.

One can identify three significant moments for the groups in recent years. There was the First National Conference on Small Christian Communities, coordinated by the Paulians (a Catholic lay movement) and held in Sydney in 1989. Then there was a National Meeting held in Sydney, 1994, and sponsored by Archbishop Leonard Faulkner. Representatives were invited from all the Catholic dioceses and 41 attended; the gathering was animated by

Fr José Marins and Sr Carolee Chanona. The issue in both of these gatherings was *the linking, or networking, of small Christian communities* and how it might be achieved. Not easy in such a vast country with its arid, and thinly-populated, heartland. Finally, there was a Brainstorm Session: *Small Christian Community in Australia* in Sydney on 29 July 1995. The aims of this encounter were:

- to bring together key people representing various small Christian community initiatives,
- to obtain a wide picture of what is happening in Australia,
- to bring into focus significant and common factors,
- to attempt an evaluation, and
- to put together any recommendations that might seem relevant.

In the event, the participants found that they had bitten off more than they could chew. They touched on the first three items, but the two remaining ones had to await deliberation at some future date. However, after 'the long silence' since the First National Encounter (1989), they felt it was perhaps time for another such meeting. The final communal reflection raised some vital issues that should exercise the minds of the communities for some time to come. The issues:

- how to cope with, and coordinate in, a situation of diversity;
- how to deal with the growing phenomenon of inclusivity;
- how to find what motivates small Christian communities; and
- how to discover the real Jesus in this world of ours.

Australian Christians would tell you that their society is one of the most secularized in the world. Added to this, like so many other wealthy nations, they face all the evils of materialism. I feel that the task of building small Christian communities is more difficult for them than for most. As such we can only be encouraged, edified, and surprised by what they are achieving. Like the United States and Canada, they of course have also to come to terms with a variety of cultures and their efforts to do so can enlighten us all.

I'm sure Australia can be enriched perhaps in a special way by what is happening in neighbouring *New Zealand* and vice versa. We learn of one such experience from New Zealand in an informative and practical book entitled *Community: Give It A Go!* by Pauline O'Regan and Teresa O'Connor. It tells of what was done by a small group of community workers in a city suburb; this story is set within the wider context of a network of small Christian communities within the parish of North East Christchurch. And casting their glance even further afield, the writers note correctly the connection between what their group is doing and the work of such secular bodies as the Picot Committees, Maori Access, and area health boards. These initiatives they would undoubtedly support.

Within the compass of Australia there is also Oceania; not without good news either. The communities are astir in Papua New Guinea. This is due in no small way to the endeavours of Fr Salvator Dougherty OFM Conv. at the St Martin's Pastoral Centre in Aitape. Even as he was dying of a brain tumour he did not stop working. Together with his religious and lay collaborators this courageous priest formed hundreds of animators for small communities down the years. Sal, who has since died, received training himself at the Kenema Pastoral Centre in Sierra Leone, while trying to convince all his friends regarding the invincibility of the All Blacks! Fr Eduardo and Sr Quentin now carry on the work.

Europe

Whether it be East or West, we encounter small Christian communities in Europe among many denominations. It may not surprise us that they exist in Western Europe, but Eastern Europe is another matter. How could they possibly have survived under Communism, we wonder. Yet they did. In 1987 Dr Ian Fraser of the Scottish Council of Churches was visiting Hungary in an effort to make contact with any groups that might be operating there. He was not having much success and was feeling quite discouraged. Then out of the blue a man walked close behind him on the street one day and asked in hushed tones, 'Do you want to make contact with basic Christian communities?' 'Yes,' replied a surprised Dr Fraser. 'Well I can put you in contact with 6,000.'

So strong were these groups that after the fall of the Berlin Wall in 1989, they considered, as one of many options, the possibility of forming a political party to work for democracy. This, however, was quickly rejected as the path for them to take as Christians. Instead they decided to support those parties and pressure groups whose values seemed most compatible with the kingdom of God. The process by which they reached their decision was important.

The whole issue was referred to the grassroots for discussion and discernment.

When the Wall came down, it may have appeared to us as miraculous. However, long before it happened there were those in East Germany who through their witness and action were making cracks in it. Not least among these were the Christian, largely Lutheran, communities, whose guttering candles lighting up hopeful faces along that obscene barrier we shall long remember. In still more oppressive circumstances, small communities survived in the former Czechoslovakia.

What might well be the earliest small Christian community in Europe began on the island of Iona, Scotland, in 1938, and is still in existence. Indeed there are groups that take their inspiration from Iona in many parts of the world. At most the island community would see themselves as a John the Baptist to the small Christian communities that have now emerged on all continents. John did not generate anything. He prepared the way. Iona would have been an early swallow heralding summer.

The connection of Iona to Columba and early Celtic monasticism is intriguing; the Celtic Church model was nothing if not communitarian. Witness all those intertwining circles in Celtic art. By the way, this is not a cryptic attempt at saying that the small Christian communities began in Ireland and Scotland!

During the 1960s there was a Catechumenate movement in France (not the Neo-Catechumenate of today) that was destined to have quite a bearing on establishing the groups in Europe. The members of the Catechumenate were rightly concerned that candidates for baptism, and indeed those already baptized, should thoroughly understand the importance of, and responsibilities arising from, the sacrament. Experience showed, however, that catechumens have to be prepared for baptism in a community environment; otherwise the newly received can soon be lost. This realization was a factor in triggering off small communities in France and the rest of Europe.

The following would have been key instants in the development of the European groups:

- The setting up in 1948 of the World Council of Churches in Geneva and the establishing of its Department of Laity.
- Vatican II with its vision of a Church that would be modelled on the

community of the Trinity (cf. *Dogmatic Constitution of the Church*, 4).

- As a result of John XXIII and Rosemary Goldie acting together , 15 representatives from the Orthodox, Protestant, and Reformed traditions were asked in 1963 to feed indirectly into Vatican II's thinking on the Church. Australian Rosemary Goldie was the executive secretary of COPECIAL, the Permanent Committee for International Congresses of the Lay Apostolate of the Roman Catholic Church, and a confidant of John XXIII on the laity. These representatives were then put in contact with 15 others from the Roman Catholic tradition for discussions.

- The following year, 1964, all the foregoing representatives met for an exchange. For about 12 years the World Council of Churches had done much reflection on the whole question of the laity. So, as from two tributaries meeting (the World Council of Churches and Rome) the notion of Church as *people of God* emerged. At this particular session there was a Catholic Mass, an Orthodox Eucharist, and a Reformed Communion Service; the latter presided over by Dr Ian Fraser who was with the World Council of Churches at the time and, incidentally, was the person who informed me of these events and, indeed, wrote about them at the time (*Gin ye daur* [Do you dare], *Scotsman*, Sept 25, 1965). The Catholic representatives noted elements in the Reformed Communion Service that they themselves were trying to recapture in their liturgical reforms. This 1964 meeting was presided over by Claus Von Bismarck of Germany, who was a Protestant. From 1964 Martin Work, a Catholic, and Ian Fraser co-chaired the sessions of this ecumenical initiative up to the Laity Congress in 1967.

- With the revolutionary year of 1968 authority everywhere felt threatened. Rome itself was alarmed by the disturbances and, according to Fraser, began to retrench.

- Given this situation the years 1969 and 70 saw a substantial increase of groups in Europe which were eager to carry on the work of Vatican II, so they began to collaborate and forge links. Firstly there were regional gatherings of small Christian communities within France, Holland, Italy, and elsewhere; then national assemblies. And finally there were European congresses in *Amsterdam 83, Turin 85, Bilbao 87,* and *Paris 91.* The progression from regional gathering to national assembly to European congress is interesting. It was prompted by the fear of relapsing into heavy top-down structures and a desire to consolidate the grassroots, where dialogue and participation were becoming the order of the day. Even before the collapse of the Berlin Wall, the European congresses had representatives from Eastern Europe; indeed they had representation from other parts of the world as well so as to acquire a more universal understanding of the groups. There is a European Collective with representatives drawn from the various countries which meets from time to time for purposes of linking and planning.

A word on the home countries. There are small communities in England and house Churches in Scotland which have been part of the European scene for quite some time. Some of them would be residential, such as Little Gidding and Post Green in England. These are also ecumenical. On the whole the efforts to establish the groups are in their very beginnings and presences are sporadic. Some of the initiatives entail restructuring of parishes; two parishes in Wales are attempting this, and there are also several Anglican parishes in Birmingham similarly engaged. In Plymouth two pastors are working towards communities along the lines proposed by José Marins, while in Leicestershire one Catholic parish has adopted the Baranowski method. Regarding courses, the College of the Ascension in Birmingham has one entitled *New Ways of Being Church*, which is fostering community development in parishes; while the RENEW programme is to be found in some Catholic dioceses. The Alpha course, which again encourages community, is also gaining in strength.

The Irish connection with Europe is more recent. Some members of a Dublin Group from Crumlin attended the Paris Congress in 1991, but didn't pretend to represent anyone except themselves. There are hundreds of prayer and faith-sharing groups in Ireland which would not consider themselves as communities, though some undoubtedly are. A small number would definitely identify themselves as such, in the Dun Laoghaire, Crumlin, and Ballinteer areas of Dublin for example. The Ballinteer experience is an effort at promoting a cell system within parishes and the Oikos movement would be doing the same. In a recent book, *Seeds of a New Church*,[19] John O'Brien CSSp points to, and reflects on, twenty-one creative pastoral initiatives in Ireland – initiatives that strive to implement the vision of Vatican II. Again in the Archdiocese of Dublin there is a team for Pastoral Development and Renewal which encourages the formation of groups throughout the archdiocese. Good work to promote small communities was also done by the Adult Education Centre, Mountjoy Square.

There would seem to be a reluctance among groups to link with one another; maybe they feel that their new found autonomy is rather fragile. They are afraid of those who might want to organize or control them from the outside. The Dublin group of which I myself am a member has tried, unsuccessfully, to link with neighbouring ones. We feel that the support would be good and local networking, for a start, helpful. The idea is not to dragoon people into anything or introduce structures, but simply to share experiences. In God's own good time we could discern where all this might lead. A more successful attempt to do this is now happily under way.

In addition to the above mentioned European Congresses there have been smaller, and therefore more personal, European Seminars held at *Innsbruck 93* and *Geneva 95*. There was the feeling that the congresses were of their very nature somewhat unwieldy and that something more reduced was also called for. In both of these gatherings there has been a greater participation of East Europeans of whom a good number have been young people. It will be helpful to say a word about what happened at the most recent seminar which took place at Geneva from 30 November to the 3 December 1995. The themes to be discussed were:

• A new way of being Church in the European situation.
• A new way of expressing the faith in an unjust world.
• How to maintain the spiritual dimension of life, while being socially committed? Or put another way: Between struggle and liturgy where do we stand?

As yet there are no official documents from the meeting. However, I feel that the resolutions of the English-speaking block cover the main points that emerged. These were summarized as follows:

The small Christian communities will be *countersigns* (go against the prevailing current) to promote:
• a culture of non-violence as against one of violence,

- an economic culture of sharing as against one of greed,
- a culture of participation as against one of exclusion,
- a culture that respects the environment as against one that destroys it.

The statement then goes on to add: these priorities will be worked out in the particular contexts in which the communities find themselves and in cooperation with all groups, whether religious or secular, that share such aspirations. Furthermore we shall give serious attention to the women issue in the light of theology and the word of God, and to the long-term organization of the communities. And, finally, we eagerly look forward to three coming events: the Synod of Christian Women to be held at Gmünden, Austria, 21-28 July, 1996; The Second European Ecumenical Assembly which will take place in Gratz, Austria, 16-18 May, 1997; and the worldwide celebration of the year 2,000, or the Millennium.

The participants at the seminar were certainly good and committed people, yet largely white and middle class. Where are the economically deprived folk? And where are people of other races? These were questions raised on many occasions.

The European small communities have in fact felt deeply challenged by Gorbachev's vision of building *One European Home* for *all* the continent's inhabitants. Not an easy task with the free market policies of the West and the ethnic wars of the East. Despite having overthrown Communism, very many Easterners are not buying into liberal Capitalism, and maybe there is a message there for all of us.

As the reader will have gathered, the European communities are ecumenically minded. While respecting each other's identity, the different denominations are quite at ease with one another and collaborate in every way they can. The Iona community, of which we spoke above, is composed of various denominations. So too is the well known Corrymeela Community that has worked so hard for reconciliation in Northern Ireland. Yet even when groups are denominational, they are still strongly ecumenical in outlook.

In their early days the European small Christian communities were somewhat alienated from the institutional Church, which they felt was dragging its feet on the reforms of Vatican II. The problem was that the Church in Europe had had an extremely long history and naturally found it hard to accommodate change.

However, despite the tensions, the groups remained within the Church, if on the margins. There would now seem to be a fresh openness on both sides and the realization that they can enrich one another. The established Churches, after all, have a tradition, history, and resources that are crucial for emerging groups.

Incidentally, some of the East European delegates at Geneva seemed to have had a much more positive experience of the official Church than their Western counterparts.

Maritime Follow-up Ministries

Not only are small Christian communities to be found on land; they are also to be found on the highseas, largely through the endeavours of the Maritime Follow-up Ministries, a movement devoted to the spiritual welfare of seafarers. There are some 300 ships, plying the waters of the world, which have Ministering Seafarer/ Fellowship Coordinators on board to foster community. These Coordinators, or Ministering Seafarers, who are themselves members of crews, are linked to some 200 chaplains in ports around the globe. The chaplains, too, network with one another and are provided with an updated list of ships and Ministering Seafarers once every three months.

The aim is to look after the physical, emotional, and spiritual needs of seafarers; the ministry is holistic, or complete. Indeed one of the major factors that sparked it off was the appalling conditions of seafarers on board many vessels, particularly those flying flags of convenience. They had no rights and were said to be treated like *campesinos* in Latin America. Great emphasis is placed on listening and caring and the use of the term *follow-up* is quite intentional. If we really care about someone, we just don't listen to their troubles once and then drop them. Those at sea receive strong backing and encouragement from the chaplains and their helpers at base. This is achieved by every possible means: letters, faxes, radio, Bible correspondence courses, the provision of audio visual materials, planning and resource centres in the ports. A beautiful and instructive aspect of this whole growing phenomenon is that it is multi-ethnic and multi-denominational.

The following were some of the significant moments for the Maritime Follow-up Ministry:

- The Meeting of the North American Maritime Ministry Association (NAMMA) in Seattle, October 1- 4, 1984 (at that time it was known as the International Council of Seamen's Agencies – ICOSA). An inter-denominational panel discussed maritime ministry, which resulted in the setting up of a multi-denominational International Coordination Committee for Maritime Follow-up Ministry (ICCMFM). Its purpose has been purely practical, namely, to coordinate the follow-up ministries with which various agencies intend to be involved. It has also given the opportunity for sharing of concerns, information, and resources between denominations and agencies in North America and worldwide.

- Personal visits made to various countries in Africa and Asia by the Tacoma [Washington State] Seamen's Center staff which provided the opportunity to discuss maritime follow-up ministry and inter-port linkage, or networking, usually with positive results.

- The Houston-based Port Chaplaincy Training School invited the Director of the Tacoma Seamen's Center to present the Maritime Follow-up Ministry Programme as part of their curriculum in 1993. This was at the specific request of the Lutheran Association for Maritime Ministry.

- An invitation by the Vatican for the Director of the Tacoma Seamen's Center to attend as an observer at the XIXth World Congress of the Apostleship of the Sea in October 1992. This provided rich opportunities to make valuable contacts and promote the concerns of the Maritime Follow-up Ministry. The Congress theme, *Christian Living Aboard Ship*, was discussed with enthusiasm and, if pursued with vigour, should give momentum to the programme of the Maritime Follow-up Ministry.

- The presentation of an account of the Maritime Follow-up Ministry to the International Association for the Study of Maritime Mission in April 1993 by the Director of the Tacoma Seamen's Center. This provided the opportunity to highlight the importance of the Maritime Follow-up Ministry programme.

The Rev Ray H. Eckhoff, who is in fact the Chaplain/Director of the Tacoma Seamen's Center (1225 E. Alexander Ave, Tacoma, Washington 98421), has with his staff played quite a part (he would downplay it) in setting up the Maritime Follow-up Ministry Programme. He makes the following hope-filled prediction:

I want to illustrate the almost incredible implications of this cooperative enterprise:

If, on the average, 50 chaplains each recruit one Ministering Seafarer/Fellowship Coordinator per week or 50 per year, then in just three years we would have 7, 500 witnessing seafarers either on the highseas or at home. Imagine how many lives would be changed by the Gospel which is the dynamite of God ... I pray that Seafarer Chaplains everywhere will see this day as the window of opportunity, the Kairos moment, for cooperation in the Maritime Follow-up Ministry.

Universal Declarations

Where small communities are concerned, there have of course been statements of a universal nature. We take note of the following:

- The Second Vatican Council 1962-'65 launched the vision of a fresh communitarian model of Church (cf. *Dogmatic Constitution on the Church*, nos. 4, 10, 11, 12).

- Interest of the World Council of Churches' Uppsala Assembly (1968) in creative Church initiatives led eventually to a world-wide contact with small Christian communities. As a result, community experiences were recorded by Dr. Ian Fraser and his late wife Margaret and are to be found in a Resource Centre at the Scottish Churches' House in Dunblane.

- The International Catechetical Congress held in Rome, 1971, cited the small community as a particularly suitable environment for passing on the faith and confirmed this in a follow-up document *General Catechetical Directory*, no. 93, 1971.

- *The Evangelization of Peoples* of Paul VI, 1975, has an entire section (no. 58) on the communities. Paul sees them as offering hope to the whole Church provided they are faithful to its teaching, united to the local and universal Churches, and avoid thinking themselves superior to other groups and movements. He also urges the members to grow as missionaries in their awareness, fervour, and zeal. And he makes the important point that the small Christian community is an authentic *cell of the Church*.

- In his *Address to the Brazilian Basic Ecclesial Communities*, 1980,

John Paul II repeats that the small communities are Church and insists on the need for their lay animators to be in communion with their pastors, prepared in the faith, and of exemplary life.[20]

• Finally, in his *Exhortation: Vocation and Mission of the Lay Faithful*, no. 28, John Paul again affirms small groups.

* * *

And so ends our historical profile. In the course of it we noted some of the key meetings held and official statements made on the subject of small Christian communities. Such events are, I believe, a sign that something important is happening among the people of God. Real history takes place at the grassroots.

Question
Do you think the history of small Christian communities is important? Why?
Suggested Bible passage: Acts 1: 15-26.

PART II

What are Small Christian Communities, and what do they do?

CHAPTER 2

Organization

In short a small Christian community is a group:

- consisting of about eight members (I would regard 30 as the absolute maximum).
- usually related to a specific area or neighbourhood, though the emphasis is on people rather than place (also found in schools, universities, and on the highseas).
- which links up with similar groupings to form a communion of communities.
- whose members believe in, and are committed to, Christ and strive to share all aspects of their lives, such as, faith, commitment, worship, ideas, intuitions, friendship, material possessions, and good works (the sharing is holistic: spiritual, intellectual, intuitive, emotional, and practical).
- who relate deeply to one another, giving witness in their unity to the harmony of the Trinity, being, in fact, body of Christ.
- that are anchored in the Eucharist, word of God, prayer, reconciliation, and reflection.
- for whom leadership is a matter of animation, coordination, and facilitation and whose decisions are made through dialogue and consensus (discernment).
- who are a leaven quietly at work among the people.
- who reach out from the reality of their unity to further the kingdom of God and its justice through mission (action) in the world.
- who make an option with the poor and live simply, as Jesus did.

Obviously we are going to have to unpackage all this.

Some people imagine that small Christian communities are composed of members who, like religious, live under the same roof. Not so. As we have already seen, there are residential groups; however, the vast majority are made up of people who live in their own houses, but gather together in a home or some other appropriate place to form community.

There are *three essential elements* really to the life of the small communities:

- bonding,
- contemplation, and
- reality.

We shall proceed to treat of these themes, dealing first of all with the reality, or practicalities, of the groups. Then later we shall turn to the more visionary, though no less important, aspects of bonding and contemplation.

Right from the outset there is one fundamental point that has to be made regarding the ordering of small Christian community. The organization is for people, not people for the organization. By this we mean that if the structures employed by a group do not help the participants in their efforts to relate to one another, they must be looked at seriously and, when necessary, changed. Persons must come first.

Where do we start?

When we come to the issue of organizing the small communities, how to start becomes a problem. First of all there must obviously be *a person or persons interested* in the idea. This person or these persons can be lay, religious, or clerical. It is not enough, however, for someone to be an enthusiast if she does not win the people at the grass-roots to her cause. Where the initiative comes from is of no great consequence. What is important is that the people make it their own. We have already seen how the suggestion first came from the bishops in Africa, but it found fertile ground among the people. Elsewhere, for example in Latin America, the push came from the rank and file.

The next principle is that *we must start from where we are*. This means that local circumstances must be carefully taken into account. If, for instance, I am trying to get groups going in Africa, I can count on a strong sense of community and family among the people. The ground is prepared and I can start directly with the work of launching the communities. This I actually saw happening in many an African situation.

In the North it can be an entirely different matter. Very often folk feel alienated and family and community are weakened. In Dublin during recent decades many residents were uprooted from communities with a long and rich tradition in the inner city to be moved to faceless suburbs where they were surrounded by strangers. The nuclear family was left to flounder without the support of gran and grandad, uncles and aunts, cousins and neighbours. This was a traumatic experience. The first task in a situation like this has to be a fostering of basic human relationships. So one would strive to bring people together on whatever basis: recreational, social, or political. At the beginning it might be just a chat and cup of coffee, and it might progress to groups getting together to obtain those amenities that sometimes are forgotten in the rush to put up more and more houses.

In Perth, Australia, Exodus, a resident small Christian community in a populous area, engaged in the task of bringing more cohesion to their district in the hope of getting some sort of neighbourhood groups going. They realized it could not be done overnight. Gradually they were making social contact with their neighbours and involving them in such activities as arts and crafts. As I remember, they also did some Bible sharing and prayer. Even in South America, where the residents in the *barrios*, or poor urban areas, are quite community-minded, I found formative courses in a variety of areas (spiritual, educational, and technical) a good means of triggering small communities.

No matter where we happen to be, when we come to the point of starting a group, the first thing required is *information*. Those who might be interested need to know something about small Christian communities, and this often leads to a course or workshop on the subject. During the workshop we can share guidelines regarding the practical workings of the communities and the vision that accompanies them. But as mentioned in our introduction, there is no neat package to unwrap. No blueprint. There are only ideas and down-to-earth suggestions that can help groups move in the right general direction. And, most importantly, everything said on a workshop has to be examined by the participants in the light of their own experience, because they have to make it flesh and blood in their own situation. The communities relate closely to the areas in which they find themselves. They cannot be transplanted unchanged from one situation to another.

If those doing the course decide they want to implement small Christian communities, they must be urged to be practical. Vague intentions are of no use at this point. What is called for are about four or five really concrete steps that will help to launch the groups. So the participants ought to be helped discern these through dialogue and the guidance of the Holy Spirit.

Last Autumn (1994) I was involved in a workshop in a Dublin parish. It ran for about two hours each Thursday over a six-week period. Thoughts regarding the vision and practicalities were duly shared and the participants examined them in the light of their own reality. Most of those who had taken part were eager to establish communities. But now there came the task of belling the cat. How were they going to establish them? They divided up into groups and discussed, discerned (allowing the Bible to shed its light), and prayed. On coming together they put forward these functional points:

- First of all they would build on existing groups trying to enrich them so that they might become small Christian communities and not remain simply groups.
- Those who were not members of any group would start their own with a view to becoming a community.
- They would emphasize the whole area of contemplation (there was an activity group to cater for every need in the parish, but they felt the spiritual backing was insufficient).
- Lastly they decided that they should manifest a special concern for the poor, the old, the handicapped, and otherwise disadvantaged members of society.

Although we have been using the word 'group' while referring to 'community' to avoid repetition, strictly speaking there is a considerable sociological difference between the two. In fact, to move from being a group to becoming a community demands something of a seachange. The divergences are as follows:

- A group has a specific purpose (e.g. to study the Bible or save the whales), whereas a community has broad interests (e.g. worship, evangelization, peace and justice, environment, youth, and so on).
- The members of a group are usually of the same age, specialization, or sex (e.g. youth or married couples); in a community on

the other hand people differ in age, social condition, race, sex, and even religious practice (in the case of an ecumenical community).

- The group is temporary, assembles for a purpose, and disbands when its objective is achieved; but a community of its nature tends to be long-term or permanent.
- The most profound distinction is that in a group the members do not necessarily have the intention of relating in depth, yet in a community they do have such an intention.
- A group is not generally a priority for its members, whereas a community most certainly is.

We do not point to these differences through a lack of appreciation for groups. Indeed, as a matter of urgency, we ought to encourage constructive groupings of all kinds, whether religious or secular. It's simply a case of pointing to the divergences that sociologists indicate.

A final suggestion for starting small Christian communities would be *to build on existing groups*, so that they are transformed into communities. The reader will remember that this was what the participants in the Dublin workshop, mentioned above, decided upon, with some success from what I have heard. One could think of a number of interest groups that could lend themselves to such a change:

- Bible study gatherings,
- RENEW groups,
- prayer, charismatic, liturgical, choral, and catechetical groupings,
- graduating classes,
- small congregations at house Masses,
- those involved in discussion or problem-solving forums,
- groups engaged in some struggle, or cause,
- participants at a workshop, programme (e.g. RCIA, Marriage Encounter), or practical task,
- fellow-workers,
- fellow students,
- ship-mates,
- close neighbours,
- persons of the same ethnic background – provided they remain entirely open to those of other ethnic origins.

In Africa it has often been:
- a core of the extended family,
- a group of the newly baptized,
- a nucleus of compound, village, or outstation.

Incidentally if one happens to be giving a workshop in a parish with the hope of starting groups, it is useful to speak about the matter beforehand during the Sunday Eucharist or services. In this talk one would share briefly what small Christian community is about, say that it might be of particular interest to those already in groups, yet welcome anyone who might be interested. This openness is important.

Yet another point. Launching one community may at times be the best we can do. It is much better, however, to begin with at least two. This makes interaction and sharing of experiences possible. Sometimes, though, persons who have been through a course or workshop form a pilot group to begin with, and learn by doing. When eventually they feel confident about running the meetings and facilitating the group, they start in their own neighbourhoods. They act as resource people. But when the neighbours are comfortable with the process, the resource person, or planned leader, allows their own animators to emerge. Indeed the major concern of the resource person should be the empowering of all the members of the community.

Finally the issue of groups sharing experiences is of the utmost importance. In our first chapter we noted how the early Christian communities did not exist in isolation. They linked together to form *a communion of communities*. Christians, either as persons or groupings, cannot isolate themselves from one another and remain Christian. We need the experience of *the intimate community*, yet equally we need the wider network, so as not to wither and die. The small Christian communities are autonomous, but not absolutely so. Occasions should therefore be sought to bring groups together in a variety of ways: for meetings, courses, and liturgical and social celebrations.

The leader's role

I was once attending a group in Southern Africa which was discussing leadership. They were critically examining the word *chairman* which is a title frequently used for the leader of a small community in that region. One person present was quite emphatic: 'To speak of the chairman of a small community is a contradiction in terms!' The consensus was for some new title that would respond better to what was required. 'I suggest that we use the word *servant* in our own language,' said a woman. 'That is what a leader is supposed to be.' The trouble with *chairman* or *chairperson* would be that historically they carry the meaning of a dominating, top-down brand of leadership. The attempt to invest the words with a new meaning would be like trying to pour new wine into the old wineskin of the chairman. So the group concluded amid laughter.

Does the problem exist to the same extent for the term *leader* itself? I am not quite sure. However one thing is certain. What the woman said about leadership being for service is pure gospel. The leader's role is *one of animation, coordination and facilitation, not of domination* (cf. Matthew 20:20-28; Mark 10:35-45; Luke 22:24-27 and John 13:1-20). In our Dublin small community we speak of *coordinators* rather than *leaders*. And instead of having one coordinator, there is a *team* of three.

There are both practical and theological reasons for this. Because of work, it may on occasions be impossible for a particular coordinator to be present, so the others continue. One of our coordinators at the moment is a nurse and her working hours are of course irregular, which means that sometimes she is unavoidably absent, or delayed. A solitary coordinator may also grow possessive of the group and begin to speak of 'my community,' whereas the group is of all. Theologically, if there is a team of animators rather than a solitary one, the principle of community is maintained even in the leadership. The motor of the community is itself a little community. And, after all, isn't the universe facilitated by a team of Three? Furthermore it is highly desirable that both male and female be represented on the coordinating group.

It is the community that is the priority and the coordinating team is there to help it function and make decisions. I have come across some groups which rotate the leadership from week to week. They said it worked for them. I wonder if it might not cause a little confusion at times. In any case the leadership in a community is usually renewed with regularity, and, if there is a team, not all the leaders are changed together. This facilitates renewal, yet at the same time assures continuity. A maximum of two years service would be common enough.

Coordinators should be chosen with care. In our community we usually devote a few meetings to the process. We dialogue so as to identify the qualities required in our animators at the time the choice is being made. We bring the word of God and prayer to bear on the issue. And then we choose. Usually with us a few names are floated and we say, 'Annette, would you mind?' or 'Andrew, how about it?' The members have been generous in accepting and nearly everyone has been a coordinator at some time or other down the years. Indeed some have been called on more than once. In other places, the members agree to go the road of a secret ballot.

Considering the qualities needed in the coordinator at a particular time is important. For the past couple of years we have had a number of new members join our group, so we felt it would be good that one of the animators should be a person with a gift for making people feel at home.

A final point on the choice of coordinators. If a group is beginning, it is a mistake to choose them too soon. The members must be given a chance to get to know each other. Usually the resource person, or planned leader, helps the group to get well off the ground before facilitators are chosen. Leaders must be given time to emerge.

In order for a group to work smoothly there are *vital inter-personal skills* that coordinators must strive to cultivate both in themselves and in the membership.[1] These are:

- *empathy* (the ability of listening to, and walking with, another),
- *personal disclosure* (an openness to the other),
- *confrontation* (challenge that is responsible and non-menacing),
- *non-defensive exploration* (a readiness to examine a situation, when challenged, without feeling we have to defend ourselves).

The coordinators must also help the group to deal with *conflict*, which is an inescapable part of the life of any community, and especially of the small Christian community where relationships are deep. Conflict doesn't mean the end of the world. It is more often a sign of health than a symptom of disease. We must be prepared to accept feelings of anger in ourselves and others and show respect for people even when we disagree with them. When we argue strongly over issues that really matter to us, we engage at deeper levels than usual. Not to care either way destroys a community much more speedily than conflict. To differ sharply can be a first step towards resolving a problem through constructive confrontation. This, for example, should be a case of inviting a member to examine some aspect of behaviour objectively rather than attacking her in a harsh judgmental way. *If we sincerely focus our attention on issues and not on persons, we can indeed avoid a great deal of tension.*

We must always deal promptly with conflict. Problems do not get better by leaving them; usually they get worse. There are skills for dealing with one another in a group that help us to overcome conflict. They are as follows:

- *clarification* (to be clear as to what exactly the problem is),
- *negotiation* (dialogue to resolve the difficulty),
- *imagination* (to seek out fresh ways of dealing with the issue),
- *celebration* (to employ liturgical and social occasions to bring about healing).

Allowing for diversity can also relieve tensions within communities. After each one of us was created, the Lord broke the mould. We are unique, reflecting God to the world in our own special way and, if we don't do it , no one else can. Of course it is not only humans who are different; we also find diversity in God, ministry, and belief, so the ability to rejoice in diversity is crucial. It would be an intolerable world if everything and everybody were the same. So the animators of groups must urge the members to live with diversity. Jesus sets the example. There is that wonderful little episode in the gospel where John comes up to him and says:

Teacher, we saw a man
casting out demons in your name,
and we forbade him,
because he was not following us.

To which the Lord replied:

Do not forbid him;
for no one who does a mighty work in my name
will be able soon to speak evil of me.
For the one that is not against us is for us.
(Mark 9:38-40; cf.also Luke 9:49-50)

Other vital tasks for the coordinators would be involving each and every member in the life and activities of the community. A judicious sharing of chores is called for here, so that some are not left free-wheeling. Special attention is of course paid to relating people to one another and fostering commitment. Liturgical and social celebration can play a great part in achieving these objectives. This we have already mentioned. The Eucharist may be central, yet a birthday should not be forgotten either.

Symbols too are important. Just last night in our Dublin community we were discussing whether religion had anything to do with nature. Dolores, the animator, had put flowers, a candle scented with eucalyptus, a book containing the story of Humpty Dumpty belonging to her little daughter Niamh, and a banana, on a small table in the centre: all to remind us that the world round about us is the sacrament, or presence of God. God is the light, little children at play, trees and flowers swaying in the wind, the food on our table ... And somehow, through employing these earthly symbols, our sharing reached depths of content and intimacy that we had rarely achieved before. Jesus anointing the eyes of the blind man with spittle suddenly took on a whole new dimension (cf. Mark 8:23). 'I feel that I have been moved on in my spiritual search by this meeting,' said Annette. 'Maybe we have all moved on.' I'm sure she was right.

Much happens in the meetings of small Christian communities and coordinators must have the ability to facilitate them. It doesn't mean that they have to conduct the sessions every time; they can delegate the work. But for whoever does it these hints may be of help:

- Try to get people to sit together and in as near to a circle as feasible.
- Ensure that eye contact between participants is possible.
- Encourage all to get involved, yet try to avoid lecturing, advice-giving, and preaching.
- Attend to body language (if people look confused, ask the speaker to clarify the point).
- Make sure the participants keep to the topic.
- Allow for diverse opinions, urging persons to consider views other than their own.
- Stress the importance of *listening*.

The fact that we discuss the role of the coordinators in communities should not distract us from the realization that it is not they, but *the community as a whole, that is the priority*. The leaders are there to serve the body. It is most difficult to free ourselves of the mindset which sees leadership in terms of domination. The coordinator offers a ministry of animation to the community. Another member may have a gift for working with young people; yet another a talent for music or liturgy. Through baptism we are a community of equals and the various members will have their *areas of competence,* which they will put at the disposal of the group. So overall coordination, or leadership in the gospel sense, would be an area of competence no greater or no less than a gift for the youth apostolate. Both build up the body of Christ. We are all part of a royal priesthood. We are a Church of leaders; put another way, we are a Church of servants.

In our own community I, *a priest,* am not on the coordinating team at present. I seem to be emerging as *a friend, guide, resource person, and unifier for the community.* They don't regard me as being above or below them, and that's fine. I see it as important to link the members to each other, to neighbouring groups, to the parish, diocese, and Church at large. I believe that, because the lay members are fully exercising their role, I am seeing my priestly identity more clearly. With the understanding of leadership that I have tried to outline, I don't feel threatened. I am a leader. We are all leaders. In fact I feel that I may have far more influence now than when I played the traditional role of priest. And I believe this is the way forward for the whole Church.

Decision-making

Decision-making in a small community is done through *dialogue and consensus* with a coordinator facilitating this process. The members sit down together in a prayerful atmosphere and calmly talk matters out so that they come to an agreement as to what to do. Decisions are normally made in line with this agreement, or consensus.

This manner of ordering affairs is achieved through conscientious, honest, and open dialogue. Force, manipulation, and unsavoury horse-trading are studiously avoided. The process is characterized by a genuine desire to discern the will of God with the guidance of the Holy Spirit; the word and prayer are brought to bear on the process. Paul VI says that it is through *trustful dialogue* in community that the will of God is discovered for a community (cf. *Evangelica Testificatio: Witness to the Gospel,* no. 25).[2] So we see the vital importance of the community meeting and of the dialogue which takes place there.

Dialogue is not simply a matter of speaking; even more so is it a matter of careful listening. It demands that we stand in the shoes of the other person. Such an ability to listen will help to prevent the members from stubbornly persisting in entrenched positions and will foster a mature spirit of give-and-take.

Nor is consensus majority rule. All the members of a group must come to an agreement. But suppose there are a couple of people who have deep reservations about some proposed course of action. What then? These owe it to the Holy Spirit, the community, and themselves to voice their opinions. Indeed assemblies have been turned right round by timely or prophetic interventions. Yet if the group, having duly considered their viewpoint, still feel that the proposed course ought to be followed, then the persons concerned must be sensitive to the direction in which the Spirit is moving the consensus.

As an example of a prophetic intervention, I would like to recall an incident that happened in West Africa. The coordinator for a community was being elected, and a man on the verge of being chosen. One of the members then remarked that the group had been speaking a lot about truly valuing its womenfolk and proposed that they elect a woman. This would have entailed quite a departure from normal practice in the locality. So voting began anew and a woman was speedily elected.

The Holy Spirit has a way of springing surprises. Last autumn (1994) I was requested to facilitate a weekend meeting for a group here in Ireland. There were some tensions among the members and it looked as if the body might be about to break up. My great hope was that it would not come to this and that unity would win the day. Before we got down to discuss, we celebrated a Eucharist, reflected on the word of God, and prayed. Then we had a lengthy sharing after which we went to lunch. Everything was going according to plan. The plan, that is, as I envisaged it. When we returned in the afternoon, events took a dramatic turn. It became clear that there were two equally valid but irreconcilable visions among the participants and that the Spirit seemed to be asking them to go their separate ways. This they did without acrimony and with a tinge of sadness. I have to admit that the Holy Spirit left me a little breathless that day.

I should like to refer to one part of the dynamic of that session which was to my mind crucial. It was the whole prayerful preparation consisting in this case of Eucharist, the word, and prayer. In my experience prayerful preparation can transform the environment in such meetings and lead to a tranquil and constructive exchange. Somewhere in the prayer there comes the realization that it is God's business we are about and not just our own.

So that is how decisions are arrived at in small Christian communities. We talk. And if there is no outcome, we talk some more. It may not seem as efficient as having cut-and-dried decisions handed down from on high, but in fact it is. Any progress made will tend to be irreversible, whereas with an authoritarian approach sooner or later we are prone to end up back on square one.

What we are searching for in discernment is of course the *will of God.* Where is it to be found? Is it existing *out there* somewhere waiting for us to come across it? Or does God so respect us that God is with us in the discernment? Are we, in other words, active partners in the process of forming God's will? In discerning we must also bear in mind that the Spirit of Jesus is in the whole community (1 Corinthians 12:27), and, consequently, it is essential to tap into the wisdom of all.

The Church is not a democracy is a refrain that is often used. Unthinkingly I feel. In a democracy 150 votes beats 149, which leaves quite a number of dissatisfied people. This would be completely unacceptable in a community where dialogue and consensus operate. So to say that the Church is not a democracy is true, because it ought to be much more democratic than a democracy. *The Church is a community* – a community I might add that is capable of the greatest sacrifices when it discerns what the Spirit is asking of it.

Ongoing formation

After they had survived their various ups and downs for a quite a number of years, I once asked a group with whom I worked in South America what it was that kept them going. The response was unanimous. It was the formation they had received and were receiving.

The word *formation* can have overtones of manipulation by others. But so too can *training, education,* or *instruction.* It is what actually happens that matters. The formation that we are talking about here is ultimately auto-formation, or formation that comes largely from within oneself. In other words the subject desires and participates actively and critically in the educational process; it is a question of self-enrichment.

Since formation in this sense can be so helpful, we must necessarily dwell on the topic. Formation begins with the establishment of a small Christian community and continues as long as the group continues. It should be formation in the fullest sense: spiritual, intellectual, intuitive, human, practical, and so forth.

Most formation comes through dialogue at meetings and casual conversation with friends. A sister in Zimbabwe told me of the mothers from Mozambique who during times of famine came over the Zimbabwean border carrying crushing loads of grass for animal fodder. These they sold to buy bread for their starving children back home and then set out on the long, wearying return journey. This moving scene is rivetted in my mind together with the lesson of love and sacrifice that it communicates. No lecture or treatise could have succeeded half so well as the image of those modern-day Christs, bearing their crosses with agonized and famished faces while they trod those eternal miles. Thus the good people with whom we meet and converse in our communities, and indeed elsewhere, are our greatest educators. The scripture says as much:

> For out of the abundance of the heart the mouth speaks.
> The good person brings good things out of a good treasure ...
> (Matthew 12:34).

Formation, therefore, comes through normal interaction. But with time the members of a community usually request a more organized approach as well. The dynamic of the group itself creates a longing for knowledge. Sometimes as a result of encounters and discussions in their places of work or study they may, for example, realize their deficiencies regarding the Bible or religious knowledge and ask for a solid grounding in either the one or the other. This provides the opportunity for a competent person (lay, cleric, or religious) to step in and meet a vital need.

Among the means for meeting such needs are:

- courses,
- workshops,

- sharing experiences with other small communities,
- retreats,
- talks,
- audio-visuals, and
- literature.

Formation can be provided in such areas as small Christian community itself, Bible, basic theology, justice and peace, catechetics, animation skills, group dynamics, counselling, and so on.

There are often pastoral centres where people can go for such courses and we also find resource persons who move about giving input to groups. There is a need for both approaches. One advantage of taking courses to the people is that entire small Christian communities can benefit from them, which is useful since the coordinating role circulates in communities. Normally individuals are selected to go to pastoral centres. These persons, however, should do courses with a view to going back and sharing all that they have learned with their groups. And it would be much better if a team of two or more were to go rather than just one person. They support each other when they return home.

Action/Reflection

One of the most formative dynamics in a small community is an ongoing action/reflection process which penetrates ever more deeply into the problem situation. The members don't simply do things mindlessly; they continually reflect on their action and then go out to perform better. In this action/reflection approach consists the so-called process of *conscientization*. Conscientization raises our awareness but with a view to changing the world.

An example may help to explain what conscientization means. A community in a South American *barrio* decided to give the poorest of the poor children a little present for a festive occasion.

Reflecting on this action at their weekly meeting, the members were happy with the way it went. But after some discussion one person remarked on the reaction of the parents. They had stood by with rather sour faces. The ingratitude of it!

None too quickly it dawned on them that maybe the parents were mortified because they themselves were not giving their own children the gifts.

So the next time there was the occasion to distribute presents, the group secretly supplied them to the mothers and fathers, who then went on to give them to the children.

In the following meeting the community agreed that this proved much more successful. However, someone then wondered why it was that those parents couldn't afford even a small gift for their children. By dint of reflection and action the community was getting to the heart of the social problem.

I often feel that the process of conscientization (action/reflection) is the planet's best university, for it certainly takes one far. Some of the most educated people regarding the world and how it functions in religious, political, social, and economic terms, whom I have met, have been poor *campesinos* (peasants) in Ecuador and factory workers on the outskirts of São Paulo, Brazil. In a real sense they were far more educated, thanks to conscientization, than some professional people whom I have encountered elsewhere. These latter could be most proficient in their calling, yet quite limited, for example, in their knowledge of the workings of society.

Implicit in the action/reflection dynamic, of course, there is a *sense of process*, or gradualness; a realization that growth doesn't happen overnight, but is the work of years. Such a realization is important for the members of small communities. True progress is neither unduly rushed nor unduly delayed. It proceeds at a proper pace.

Practically this means that the group:

• takes people where they are,
• challenges them to grow,
• and strives to create the environment of love and acceptance that alone makes growth possible.

When we proceed in this way, we are only imitating the manner in which God deals with all of us. The Almighty accepts and loves us as we are, challenges us through the gospel to grow, and wills for us a loving Christian family and community to help us in our endeavours. So God is most respectful of the person and we must be the same. Without the rain of acceptance and the sunshine of love we cannot mature as human beings.

This total development as persons, already referred to, is the important thing; the meetings, courses, retreats, and similar activities are to achieve this end. Above all, there has to be a gradual growth in faith and commitment, or a spiritual maturing, as happens with time in community.

In the Western world of microwave ovens and instant everything, we can easily lose our sense of process. Ours is in fact an instant society. Efficiency is at a premium: 'We have no time to stand and stare' (Davies). It is not so in the economically poorer nations. I recall visiting a chief in Zambia, who, it transpired, had lost his eldest son to a crocodile in the dark river near his compound only three weeks before. Grieving though he was, he insisted on seeing me. We of course talked about his terrible loss, but then he went on to enquire about my work. I told him that I was trying to promote small communities among Christians. He himself was not a Christian, yet politely asked how it was all going. Very slowly, I told him. He was silent for a long while, and then cited a proverb of his people: *When God cooks, there is no smoke.*

Instant coffee there may be. But there are no instant communities.

A simple Rule of Life

Some small Christian communities have a simple Rule of Life. As an example I should like to quote that of the Little Gidding group in England. This is a residential community, Anglican in its origins, but now ecumenical in its membership. This Rule asks the members:

- to pray together once a day,
- celebrate Communion and, if possible, share a meal with other community members at least once a week,
- to commit time and resources to God's service,
- and aim to live peaceably with God and others.[3]

These items are simple undertakings, not vows. And they are not meant to be cast-iron, but flexible. This flexibility is indicated by the words 'if possible'and 'for those who are able,' which are often on the lips of the group members.

Membership of a community involves certain things, such as:

- being together,
- worshipping together,
- sharing lives and goods,
- and reaching out to others (especially to those who are pushed

aside or totally excluded) on behalf of, and inspired by, the community.

The participants do their best about these requirements in accordance with circumstances.

Most communities that I meet do not have an expressed rule like Little Gidding. Our home-based Dublin group does not have one. Implicitly there are shared understandings and the essential bonding, contemplation, and reality. These, however, have not been formalized into a set of stated commitments. This would be the case with most neighbourhood groups around the world. I don't see, though, how having four or five broad-based undertakings could do anything but good. It would provide focus. I shall certainly be taking the matter up with our community.

Action

A small Christian community must be involved in action. But what action? First of all the members, *simply by being what they are* ought to bring gospel values, which are simply basic human values, to those places where their daily activities take them: the teacher to the school, the nurse to the hospital, the young person to the youth club, the politician to parliament, the factory worker to the factory, the business person to the shop. In *Populorum Progressio* (*Fostering the Development of Peoples*) Paul VI calls on Roman Catholics the world over, 'without waiting passively for orders or directives, to take the initiative freely and to infuse a Christian spirit into the mentality, customs, laws and structures of the community in which they live.'[4] This amounts to an excellent strategy for building the kingdom of God in the world.

In other words, the Church must be *in history* and not cut off from it. Too often we have erected barriers between faith and practice, religion and life, the Church and history. A story of a novice from my own seminary days illustrates this mentality. He fell ill in the course of his novitiate and the doctor was summoned. The doctor was a large good-natured man who professed no religion. I suppose he was agnostic. He enquired of the novice if he had ever had the illness before. To which the novice replied that he had had 'a touch of it' when he was *in the world*. There was a long baffled silence as the doctor tried to come to terms with this novicespeak.

Then he casually asked, 'As a matter of interest, where the devil do you think you are now?'

Not only will the members of small Christian communities witness to gospel values in their own places of study, work, or leisure, but they will also take their skills back to their homes and neighbourhoods. If someone is a nurse and a neighbour's child is ill, he will call to see if something can't be done. In reality members get involved in a whole welter of activity: providing religious education, working with young people, conducting courses, visiting the sick and those with problems, comforting those stricken with AIDS, engaging in development work, being active on behalf of the little people whom society pushes aside or excludes as being of no account. It could be, of course, that in some highly pressurized societies, the best members can do is to strive to be truly Christian at work, at home, and in the neighbourhood. But they are doing what is most important – the heart of the matter.

I think it is helpful if a group has a *plan of action*. Certainly the members ought to do something in the name of the community, and be accountable for what they do. The purpose of this is not that the group may be able to check on its members, rather is it a matter of providing an opportunity for affirming and supporting them. When they can talk about their difficulties and are upheld by the prayers and concern – even the active assistance – of their friends, it is of enormous help.

And if it be possible for them to work in teams and not just as individuals, so much the better. Jesus sent out his apostles on mission two by two, not alone. 'For,' as he says in Matthew's gospel, 'where two or three are gathered in my name, there am I in the midst of them' (18:20; cf. also Matthew 10:5-15; Luke 10:1-20).

In the complicated world of today it is not usually possible for the members of a community to be engaged in the same task. If on occasions, however, they can all join together in doing something, it is a marvellous help towards developing community. From time to time our group is called upon by the parish to help with a bucket collection for some worthy cause. A warm atmosphere always prevails and it is a wonderful chance for bonding. Indeed all the work done in the name of the grouping, whether by teams or individuals, contributes greatly to creating a community spirit.

In the beginning a community will respond to some obvious

needs round about it. With time, as it grows in maturity, the members may become more thoroughgoing in their approach. This could entail making an analysis of their area in an effort to get at the problems as seen by the ordinary people of the place. We are now talking serious pastoral planning which is an issue we shall deal with in chapter 4.

Action, of course, is buttressed by prayer, or contemplation. *The spirituality of the small Christian community is an integral one that combines prayer and outreach.* Neither aspect is neglected and this is important, because a spirituality that tries to function either on the basis of prayer or action alone is a spirituality trying to fly on one wing. Sooner or later it will splutter and crash. In a lecture in the United States I once heard Daniel Berrigan say that prayer which did not issue in action was spurious. And Teresa of Avila used to declare, 'The Lord walks among the pots and pans.'[5] And finally, although a monk, Thomas Merton was one of the first to sense that there was something awfully wrong with the Vietnam War, and condemn it. He wrote:

> But 'no man is an island.' A purely individualistic inner life, unconcerned with the sufferings of others, is unreal. Therefore my meditation on love and peace must be realistically and intimately related to the fury of war, bloodshed, burning, destruction, killing that takes place on the other side of the earth.[6]

These people are mystics. We might have a vision of them as being somewhat up in the clouds. Not so. Indeed their words show that the step from mysticism to social concern is a short one. They were truly in touch with reality.

Reality is what we have been about in this chapter – reality in terms of the organization of small Christian communities and also in terms of their outreach to build God's kingdom in this poor troubled world of ours.

Summary

(1)   Confer p. 44 for a brief description of small Christian community.
(2)   The essential elements of the life of small Christian communities are: bonding contemplation, and reality; we start with reality.
(3)   Organization is not more important than people.

(4) Small community starts:
  • with an interested person or interested persons,
  • from where we are,
  • with the necessary information,
  • possibly by building on existing groups.

(5) The experience of intimate group is necessary, yet equally that of networking, or being a communion of communities.

(6) Leadership is for service (cf. Matthew 20:20-28; Mark 10:35-45; Luke 22:24-27; John 13:1-20).

(7) The leader's role is one of animation, coordination, facilitation, not domination.

(8) Better a team (of three?) coordinators rather than one, for practical and theological (Trinitarian) reasons.

(9) The community, not the coordinating team, is the priority; it proposes and disposes facilitated by the coordinators.

(10) There are interpersonal skills vital for the running of community: empathy (ability to listen), personal disclosure (openness), confrontation (responsible challenge), non-defensive exploration (examining issues without fear).

(11) To deal with inevitable conflict the following are needed: clarification (to be clear where the problem lies), negotiation (dialogue), imagination (fresh ways of proceeding), celebration (liturgical and social).

(12) Allowing for diversity also relieves tension.

(13) Coordinators should involve members in the activities of the group and foster relationships by using celebrations (e.g. Eucharist, birthdays) and symbols (e.g. a garland or bunch of flowers to show appreciation).

(14) The priest or pastor in a small Christian community is a friend, guide, resource person, and unifier; not into control.

(15) The will of God for a community is discovered through 'trustful dialogue' (discernment) in the group (Paul VI, *Evangelica Testificatio: Evangelical Witness*, no. 25).

(16) There must be initial and ongoing formation (understood as auto-education, or self enrichment) in the small community; formation in the fullest sense: spiritual, intellectual, intuitive, human.

(17) One of the most enriching factors in the group is the action/ reflection procedure that it adopts – the process of conscientization.

(18) A small Christian community must develop a sense of process – the realization that growth is gradual and can neither be unduly rushed nor unduly delayed. It involves taking people where they are, challenging them to grow, and striving to create the environment of love and acceptance that makes growth possible.

(19) A simple Rule of Life, or four or five broad-based commitments, may be of help to a community.

(20) The spirituality of small Christian community is integral, or one; it has two facets: prayer and action.

(21) Having a plan of action can be helpful.

Questions

(1) Taking your own situation into account, have you any ideas as to what practical steps you might take to go about starting small Christian communities?
Suggested Bible passage: Mark 1: 14-28.

(2) What does leadership mean for you and your group?
Suggested Bible passage: Matthew 20: 20-28; or John 13: 1-20.

(3) How are decisions made in your community?
Suggested reading: Luke 2: 41-52;
Paul VI. *Evangelica Testificatio: Evangelical Witness*, no. 25 (cf. *Vatican II*, Flannery, 1980, fifth printing, p.692).

(4) Is formation a concern for your community?
Suggested Bible passage: Ephesians 4: 7-16.

(5) What action does your group take?
Suggested Bible passage: Isaiah 29: 12-14; or James 2: 14-26.

CHAPTER 3

Meetings

I once saw an intriguing poster which was completely filled with the heads of turkeys looking expectantly in all directions. The caption underneath read: *Now that we're organized, what do we do?* This reminds me of a problem often posed by people who hope to launch small Christian communities. 'Right,' they say, 'we want to start a small community. We come together. Now what do we do? What are the meetings like?' Let us say straightaway that there is *no cut-and-dried answer* to this question. No fixed agenda.

The essential components of the meetings are:

- bonding,
- contemplation,
- reality.

In other words the essentials of the meetings of the communities do not differ from the essentials of their life. If we are talking about community, there has to be the efforts at *bonding*, because of the intention to relate at some depth. And if the group is Christian, *contemplation* has to form a major part of its vision. When I speak of contemplation, I am not using the word in its strictly mystical sense. For me it embraces the Eucharist, word of God, prayer (all forms), reconciliation, and reflection. Finally, of course, the groupings must *do* something. They can't just focus on their internal organization and dynamics; there must be *action*, or outreach (*reality*).

The meeting of the small Christian community ought to be relevant, respond to needs. At the moment in my country, Ireland, the burning issue is the peace process in the North. This should figure in the meetings. In fact a young couple from our Dublin group travelled on a peace train to Belfast, taking their baby girl with them, in the tense days proceeding the process. Stones were thrown at the train, yet peace dawned. The other evening our community took part in a candle-light vigil outside the Nigerian Embassy here in

Dublin demanding that the life of Ken Saro-Wiwa and his companions be spared. Shamefully, the plea fell on deaf ears. It might be that a group needs to plan something, and the meeting is devoted to this. Or they might feel the desire, as our group often does, for a spiritual fillip and devote an entire meeting to prayer or the Eucharist. Needs decide the agenda of a meeting; there ought to be no rigid pattern. This doesn't mean that sessions are unplanned. Quite the contrary. In fact the preparation has to be more thorough than when there is a regular format. Generally at the end of a meeting the participants decide the subject of the next.

A group of course may want to have an ongoing theme for those moments when nothing of urgency presents itself. To go systematically through a book like this one, dealing with the questions provided, could be a help in such a situation. Or it might be a document of Vatican II like *Apostolicam Actuositatem, Decree on the Apostolate of the Lay People*.

When a group clings to some fixed methodology, it can lose out on relevance. There are suggested methods for reflecting on the Bible (one is provided in the course of this chapter) which need careful handling. The members can spend so much time on the method that they don't get round to talking about life or its problems at all. And this despite the fact that most methods rightly insist that the word of God must be related to life and put into practice, providing for this in their procedures. If this recommendation is ignored, then communities can become simply Bible-discussion and prayer groups.

There is also a practice, which is common enough, of reflecting week by week on the gospel of the following Sunday. This has the advantage that the faithful have already thought of the reading in advance and can, therefore, derive more fruit from the homily at Mass. But in terms of the life of small Christian communities I would have reservations about the routine. The Sunday gospel in question may have little to say to Wednesday's rioting. We can end up with the anomaly that the scripture, instead of being a conduit to life, is a barrier to it. The watchwords then are *relevance, flexibility, and adaptability*.

No matter what shape the sessions take, however, we ought never lose sight of *the essentials: bonding, contemplation, and reality*. These ingredients must always be part of the mix.The emphasis or order in which they come may vary, but they should always be present.

When we think of meetings, formal gatherings usually come to mind. Yet our lives are made up of rather more casual encounters. relaxed meetings at work, running into friends on the street, a game of cards or chess, study groups, meetings to prepare or celebrate the sacraments, cultural or religious functions, outings, holidays, and pilgrimages. All these can help considerably in forming community. We should be aware of this. Indeed when members reflect on factors that keep them together over long periods, apart from spiritual considerations, *purely social encounters* are very much to the fore. But, then, Christ himself loved to sit and eat and chat with people. And he provided the drinks for what must have been one of the earliest recorded cocktail parties!

Before I proceed to give some models for meetings of small communities, let me say that there are no great difficulties involved. All over the world today quite simple people will:

- sit down together,
- share the joys and problems of life,
- see what light the word of God sheds on their situation,
- consider what can be done in the circumstances,
- and pray with one another.

This is an *ordinary format* that anyone could use. Doesn't it get a bit monotonous? Not really. If we tune into a group that has been a long time on the road, we shall realize why. It is the *ever-deepening relationships* and *content* that give variety. Our Dublin group has now been going 14 years, and its last meeting was possibly the most profound and exciting I have ever attended for the reasons I have just mentioned. That doesn't mean to say that some meetings can't be humdrum. You just never know when you are going to be surprised by the Spirit, and it is well worth all the waiting.

Sample meetings

Despite having stressed the importance of flexibility, I am aware that the organizing of sessions can present some difficulty for groups, especially in their early stages. I now give a sampling of some 22 gatherings that may be of help to communities. The intention is that they may serve as examples, or paradigms, to spark off possibilities in the mind of the group facilitator, not that they be adhered to exactly. Various of them deal with topics that are important for an understanding of small Christian community, such as, unity, commitment, kingdom, contemplation, dialogue, leadership, communication, planning, evaluation. They are in note form and largely *derived from meetings that have actually taken place*.

Meeting 1: An Exercise
Theme: Relationships/Community
The basis of this meeting takes the form of an exercise, or group dynamic, to help the members of a community *relate to one another*. I have had extremely good feedback on this session. It is especially good when a group is in its initial phase, and efforts are being made at bonding.

Before launching into this dynamic, there are some points that I should like to make about sharing in general where small Christian communities are concerned. No pressure is ever exercised in small communities to get people to reveal themselves. While openness is desirable, it is completely up to people to reveal as much or as little of themselves as they wish. We must remember that persons differ greatly in this respect, and no one should say or do anything with which he feels uncomfortable. It would be a mistake for one to wear his heart on his sleeve early in the life of a group, before it has coalesced as a community. If members are going to open their hearts, they need the support of a community that they can trust. This trust grows slowly over the years.

In our own community we can share quite deeply now, and there's absolutely no problem about it. At no time in fact has it been an issue. We know one another well; are like an intimate family. Still, after 14 years, some are better than others at sharing about themselves. Anyway mostly we talk about community matters. And the community is not our spiritual director. What I'm trying to say is that it would be a mistake for someone to shy away from becoming a member of a small community because of a fear of sharing, because it is always done in a most sensitive way.

(1) The Exercise
(a) The animator of the meeting asks all present to think about the question: *Who am I?* (10-15 minutes).

(b) Each member is asked *to seek out a person* whom he does not
know or would like to know better. The pair introduce, and chat
with each other about, themselves. They will, it is hoped, reveal
something of their *feelings*. When we say how we feel about
something, people get to know us better: our feelings are our
own, our thoughts may be those of Aristotle. Interesting details
can add spice. I once talked to a girl in her teens who had done a
parachute jump for charity. I'd think twice before jumping off a
three-foot wall. The two also discuss what they would like to
gain from being in community (10-15 mins).

(c) The leader calls upon the twosomes to join other pairs so as to
make *groups of four*. The participants introduce and chat not
about themselves this time, but regarding their partners of the
previous step. Points of interest about persons are noted, and
they are asked to decide as a group what their expectations of
small community are (15-20 mins).

(d) The groups of four now combine to form *groups, or a group, of
eight*. Then each chooses a person to animate the proceedings
and a secretary to take notes. The introductions are repeated in
this larger grouping. Again the participants present their part-
ner of step (b), noting any interesting detail. They share the
expectations of community as decided upon in the groups of
four, and they choose *four expectations* which they consider the
most important. And finally they select a name for their band of
eight (15-20 mins).

(e) All now join in *a general forum* but the groups of eight stay
together. The secretary gives the name of the grouping, introduces its members, noting interesting points, and says what
their four chosen expectations are. These are written up on a
blackboard or on posters and discussed (15-20 mins).

(2) Suggested Bible passage: Acts 4: 32-37.
Having seen how the scripture might shed light on the discussion, the assembly decides on *some very practical outcome* from
their session; not simply a promise to pray for one another, for
example, important though this undoubtedly might be.

(3) There is now spontaneous prayer, or prayer that comes straight
from the heart, using one's own words (may include hymns,
chanting and music – a guitar may prove useful, or recordings).

Note: The above exercise follows the pattern of human relationships. First we are alone. Then we open to another (mother), to a limited group (the family) and finally to the whole community. Exercises or group dynamics can be a fruitful source for meetings.

* * *

Meeting 2: Simple Exercise
Theme: Community/Sharing
(1) The members place themselves in the presence of God (pause in silence).
(2) Each relates some happy event from his life, saying something of how he *felt.*
(3) Suggested Bible passage: Luke 2: 1-20.
   Does this passage shed any light on your sharing?
(4) What *action* might the group take as a result of sharing experiences and the word of God?
(5) Shared Prayer (cf. Meeting 1, 3).

* * *

Meeting 3: Simple Exercise
Theme Community/Sharing
(1) The members place themselves in the presence of God (pause in silence).
(2) Each one relates some sad event from his life, saying something about how he *felt.*
(3) Suggested Bible passage: Matthew 11:28-30.
   Does this passage shed any light on the sharing?
(4) What *action* might the group take as a result of sharing experiences and the word of God?
(5) Shared prayer (cf. Meeting 1, 3).

* * *

Meeting 4: Simple Exercise (dynamic)
Theme: Unity
(1) *Check-in:* The group may wish to share with one another regarding how things have gone for them since their last meeting. This is a possibility for opening most sessions.
(2) The animator produces a bundle of twigs bound together and invites various members to break them. If there are enough of

them this proves impossible. The facilitator then unties the bundle and asks them to try breaking them individually. This
proves a very easy task.

(3) The members then discuss the exercise and its relevance to their
lives.

(4) Suggested Bible passage: Matthew: 12: 22-28.
Does this passage shed light on the discussion?

(5) The group decides on some *action* resulting from their sharing.

(6) Shared prayer (cf. Meeting 1, 3).

* * *

Meeting 5: Worship/Bible Reflection
Theme: Community
N.B. This session is devoted entirely to a Bible reflection and a six-point
method for doing this is provided. The Bible passage under consideration:
John 17: 20-26.

(1) Invite those present to place themselves in the presence of God
(pause in silence).

(2) Ask for a volunteer to read the passage and leave a couple of
minutes for the members to think about it. Don't fear the silence;
it gives the Spirit a chance to speak.

(3) Read the extract a second time (different reader) and pause once
more for three to five minutes.

(4) Invite the participants to share regarding what the passage says
to them as individuals, paying particular attention to the challenges it raises for their lives. There should be no preaching to
others.

(5) Determine the *practical application* of the passage for the lives of
the participants. What action are they going to take? It may not
always be a question of doing something new, but of intensify-
ing some action already being taken.

(6) Shared prayer (cf. Meeting 1, 3).

Note: Needless to say, this method can be applied to any scripture
passage.

* * *

Meeting 6: Worship
Theme: Need for prayer /reflection
(This session is taken from notes that I made of an encounter in our Dublin
community some years ago.)

(1) Check-in (cf. Meeting 4, 1).

(2) The animator announced that the bulk of the meeting would be
devoted to personal reflection and prayer. A selection of stimu-
lating reading was placed on a table. A letter supposedly from
Jesus Christ was set up in one corner of the room with a few
colourful votive candles near it. In the letter Christ reminded the
reader of the personal friendship between them and wondered
if in the hurly-burly of life he found time to talk with him. The
members were free just to sit and meditate, browse through the
material provided, go read the letter, or visit a nearby chapel.

(3) After about 45 minutes the members were asked if they might
not like to share something with the community. One participant said that in the course of the meditation she thought of the
people she loved and of those who loved her. Often in daily
dealings with them she became overly aware of their faults; the
meditation restored a proper perspective, so that she saw the
goodness more clearly. A second member said that she felt
relaxed and happy. A third informed us that he had spent the
whole of the previous evening discussing God with friends. On
reflection, however, he realized that the only one whose words
were not considered in the dialogue was in fact God. Again he
said that the meeting put things in perspective. And so it went.

(4) The scripture reading was from Ecclesiastes 3:1-9 ('For everything there is a season...'). The members reflected that in the
welter of activities that went to make up their daily lives they
would have to be careful not to forget their Friend, God/Jesus.
There must be the restoring moments in order to go to the
mountain top or desert place and get a true perspective on what
really matters in life. The session gradually wound to a close in a
mixture of reflection and prayer.

* * *

Meeting 7: Worship/Eucharist
When a group devotes a session to the celebration of the Eucharist,
the important thing is the preparation. If this is done thoroughly,

the celebration usually goes well. Items to be prepared:
- the place of celebration,
- music and hymns,
- things to be celebrated; the members are asked to be ready to announce at the beginning of the Eucharist items which they wish to celebrate (e.g. 'I would like to celebrate the friendship that I find in this group'),
- readings and bidding prayers and who are going to do them,
- offertory procession (including what symbols?),
- mime at the offertory (?),
- communion reflection.

After the celebration of the Eucharist a cup of tea and some biscuits can be symbolic of the New Testament *agape*, or meal-fellowship. If something is taken following a meeting, it should always be kept simple. In some parts of the world people are so deprived that providing even tea or coffee can be financially too much of a burden. So we must be sensitive not to embarrass folk.

* * *

Meeting 8: Worship
Theme: Reconciliation
(1) Check-in (cf. Meeting 4, 1).
(2) Participants place themselves in the presence of God (silent pause).
(3) Examination of Conscience:
- Do I love my neighbour without laying down conditions for my love?
- Do I pay attention to my spiritual life?
- Am I just (i.e. are my relationships right) at home, in the community, and with people in general?
- Do I make an option with the poor and am I compassionate towards the disadvantaged?
- Am I open to others?
- Am I open to change?
- Do I put the word of God into practice?
- Do I strive to live at peace with others overcoming all obstacles in the way of doing so?
- Does failure worry me, or do I see it as a possible step towards a new beginning?

(4) Suggested Bible passage: John 8: 1-11.
    Does this reading shed any light on the reconciliation process?
(5) Act of sorrow recited in common.
    (If a priest is present, some may wish to confess privately at this
    point.)
(6) The members make a private resolution of amendment and are
    encouraged to keep it as down-to-earth as possible, not vague.
    The group may wish to make a purpose of amendment on some
    point as a community.
(7) As a symbol of conversion the participants might want to write
    down their faults secretly on a piece of paper and then proceed
    to burn them in some *safe* container.
(8) Shared prayer (cf. Meeting 1, 3).
(9) A sign of peace is shared by all.
Hymn: *Peace is flowing like a river* (?)

* * *

Meeting 9: Ordinary format (cf. p. 69 for details)
Theme: Commitment
(1) Check-in (cf. Meeting 4, 1).
(2) The members are asked to share on what commitment, or total
    dedication, means to them in their lives.
(3) Suggested Bible passage: Luke 9: 57-62.
    Does this reading shed any light on the discussion?
(4) The group decides on the *action* it will take.
(5) Shared prayer, (cf. Meeting 1, 3).

* * *

Meeting 10: Worship
Theme: Commitment
Follow the same method for Bible-sharing given in Meeting 5,
reflecting on the following passage: Mark 10: 17-31.

* * *

Meeting 11: Ordinary format (cf. p. 69 for details)
Theme : The Kingdom of God
(1) The members place themselves in the presence of God (silent
    pause).
(2) Check-in (cf. Meeting 4, 1).

(3) Suggested Bible passages: Matthew 6:33; Matthew 13: 1-33.
What do these extracts tell us about the kingdom of God and its members?
(4) What does each participant personally consider the kingdom of God to be?
(5) What practical impact can our understanding have on our lives and outreach to others?
(6) Shared prayer (cf. Meeting 1, 3.)

* * *

Meeting 12: Simple exercise
Theme: The Kingdom of God
(1) The members place themselves in the presence of God (silent pause).
(2) Check-in (cf. Meeting 4, 1).
(3) Take the understanding of the kingdom as being wherever we find *harmony rooted in justice*. Then ask the participants to think of experiences, incidents, or stories from their own lives that would illustrate this.
(4) Suggested Bible passage: Matthew 18: 23-35.
What light does this shed on the reflection?
(5) The group decides on some practical outcome to their discussion.
(6) Shared prayer (Meeting 1, 3).

* * *

Meeting 13: Group Dynamic
Theme: Animation/Leadership
(1) The members place themselves in the presence of God (silent pause).
(2) Check-in (cf. Meeting 4, 1).
(3) The dynamic is as follows:
• The participants are are invited to stand in V formation with the animator of the session at the point of the V.
• All hold hands.
• The animator/leader proceeds to move while trailing everybody else after her.
• Next the group is assembled in a huddle and the leader endeavours to push them all forward.
• Lastly they assemble in a line and, encouraged by the leader/ani-

mator, move forward shoulder to shoulder on their own steam.
(4) The members are now asked to decode, or explain, the exercise.
    Are there any implications for leadership?
(5) Suggested Bible passage Matthew 20: 20-28.
    Does the passage shed light on the discussion?
(6) Some *action* to be decided upon, resulting from the foregoing
    reflections.
(7) Shared prayer (cf. Meeting 1, 3).

* * *

Meeting 14: Group Dynamic
Theme: Coordination/Leadership
(1) The members place themselves in the presence of God (silent
    pause).
(2) Check-in' (cf. Meeting 4, 1).
(3) Here I would suggest a washing of the feet ceremony as hap-
    pens on Holy Thursday, while some appropriate hymn is being
    sung; a group coordinator to do the washing.
(4) The members are asked to comment on the significance of the
    exercise.
(5) Suggested Bible passage: John 13: 1-11.
    Does the passage speak to the issue on which the group is shar-
    ing?
(6) What *action* can be taken in the light of the reflections?
(7) Shared prayer (cf. Meeting 1, 3).

* * *

Meeting 15: Ecumenical
Theme: Ecumenical Outreach
The following is an account of a session which I had with a small Buddhist
community in a boathouse on the River Kwai just below the historic
bridge.
(1) First of all as a guest I shared a simple vegetarian meal with the
    community. Indeed it seemed to me that simplicity of lifestyle
    was for them essential to holiness. I could only guess what they
    must have thought of the affluent North.
(2) After the meal we sat together exchanging ideas and experi-
    ences. I learned about their reverence and concern for creation,
    peace and justice, a wholesome education, a world that would

not be plagued by consumerism and all its attendant ills. They were interested in what I had to say about small Christian communities (I was just returning from working in Australia). I told them that their concerns were also concerns for the Christian communities. I assured them that Christianity did not regard itself as the only path to God, but respected all religions and upheld freedom of conscience. A thing that struck me was the genuine respect of the young people present for their elders. It is something very precious that has been undermined in the North with dire consequences. As a young mother in our Dublin community once put it, 'If respect goes, everything goes.' This value needs recapturing, urgently. However, the opposite is also true; if adults are to receive respect from the youth, they must merit it. Furthermore they themselves must be careful to reverence the young.

(3) We talked long over these issues as the bright moon rolled out a glittering carpet across the River Kwai.

(4) Afterwards we sat for a considerable time in silent meditation together. I prayed to God that all their endeavours to build a better world would be blessed.

(5) Finally we dispersed and I settled down on the deck of the boathouse to sleep. They made sure to provide me with a mosquito net so that I could have an undisturbed night's rest.

* * *

Meeting 16: Ecumenical
Theme: Strength in weakness
This session took place in a retirement home in Toronto. There were eight members present (an Anglican, Baptist, Greek Orthodox, Lutheran, Pentecostal, Presbyterian, and two Roman Catholics).

(1) *Coordinator:* May the grace of Our Lord Jesus Christ, the love of God, and the fellowship of the Holy Spirit be with you all, now and forevermore.
All: Amen.

(2) *Check-in:* They all relate how they have been since their last weekly meeting. A check-in is normally brief, yet in the context of the retirement home it proved somewhat lengthy. The opportunity *to be listened to* seemed deeply valued.

(3) The previous week a lady had pointed out how hard she found

it to be charitable to an irritating neighbour. This led to the choice of the theme, *Strength in weakness*, for the current session.

(4) Bible extract chosen: 2 Corinthians 12: 5-10.

The members shared experiences of weakness and how God helped them in their debility. There was a great deal of scriptural reminiscing: a Finnish lady fondly recalling Sunday school back in her homeland when she was a little girl.

(5) They resolved to strive to be patient and kind despite their infirmities.

(6) *Shared prayer.* The participants concluded by praying for the chaplain, care staff, and patients, especially for Margery who was at death's door. They thanked God for a variety of things: the lovely Sunday service they had had, the arts and crafts class, the sing along. Then Mabel declared: 'It's wonderful how all of us, though of different denominations, can discuss and worship so marvellously together. This meeting is the highlight of my week.'

* * *

Meeting 17: Prophetic (i.e. deals with a justice issue. The prophets were greatly involved with justice issues).

Theme: This session took place in an African group. The issue was a poorly maintained road in a township.

(1) The participants said a short prayer invoking the help of the Holy Spirit in their sharing.

(2) The problem of the road was hotly debated. It seemed that its condition was so appalling that a small child nearly drowned in one of the potholes.

(3) Bible passage chosen: Luke 3: 1-6.

This passage speaks about the 'rough ways being made smooth.' If the way for Jesus is to be properly prepared, the paths must be straight. There must be no crookedness, a member said. Justice was required.

(4) *Action:* They decided to protest by going in a delegation to the municipal council bringing a list of signatures with them from the residents of the area.

(5) The shared prayer had a scriptural ring about it making use of expressions like 'making the rough ways smooth.'

Meeting 18: Prophetic/Miscellaneous: a meeting can be built on a poem,
song, reading from any source etc.
Theme: Justice (Environment)
(Yesterday I was walking in a neighbouring park, taking a break from
writing this book, when I came across a sight that greatly distressed me.
There was this glorious, shapely ash tree that must have been growing for
thirty years or more, and in a matter of minutes some vandals had cut a
circle of bark from it, assuring it of a slow, wilting death. My friend and I
were outraged at the wantonness of this. I then returned to my work and
thought up the following meeting that I hope I may be permitted to use in
our community.)

(1) The members place themselves in the presence of God (silent
    pause).
(2) Check-in (cf. Meeting 4, 1).
(3) The following poem to be distributed and the participants asked
    to ponder it for some minutes, even to commit it to memory:

I saw with open eyes	I saw in a vision
Singing birds sweet	The worm in the wheat,
Sold in the shops,	And in the shops nothing
For people to eat,	For people to eat
Sold in the shops of	Nothing for sale in Stupidity
Stupidity Street.	Street.

(4) The group then discusses the incident referred to above together
    with the poem and tease out their implications.
(5) Suggested Bible passages to choose from: Genesis 1:1-31 ('And
    God saw that it was good.'); Matthew 6:28-29 ('Consider the
    lilies of the field...').
(6) What *action* can be taken as a result of the reflections that might
    protect the environment and bring home to the perpetrators the
    harm they are doing? The thought occurred to me that we
    should start a little project to clean up the park and plant some
    trees, and we could involve the youth and children of the area in
    doing this. If a child were to plant a tree, it would surely make a
    difference.
(7) Shared prayer (cf. Meeting 1, 3). As part of this prayer, Joyce
    Kilmer's *Trees* could be read.

* * *

Meeting 19: Planning
Theme: Justice
A big fiesta is approaching, and the members of a small Christian community in a populous South American barrio want to do something to make it a memorable occasion. We have already referred to this experience in another context.

(1) The participants say a few short introductory prayers.
(2) Many ideas are put forward as to what they might do for the feast. Eventually they decide that they are going to give a small gift to the poorest of the poor children of the *barrio* (deprived area in a city). Then some members volunteer to seek sponsors so as to raise funds to purchase the gifts; others undertake to wrap them and decide who are to receive them; and finally the group decides to distribute them on the eve of the feast at the parish centre.
(3) Bible passage chosen: Acts 20:32-35 ('more blessed to give than receive').
    It certainly spoke to the situation.
(4) Shared prayer (cf. Meeting 3, 1). Hymn: *Caridad y comprensión* (*Love and understanding*).

* * *

Meeting 20: Evaluation
Theme: Justice
(After the fiesta the community evaluates its action)

(1) Jorge plays the guitar and the members sing *Santa Maria del Camino*:

> While you journey through life
> You are never alone.
> With you on the road
> Dear Mary goes.
> Although your footsteps
> Seem useless,
> You forge a path as you go;
> Now others will follow on,
> Now others will follow on.

(2) The community now evaluated the whole episode of giving the gifts to the children. They felt it had gone well. It was satisfying to help the little ones, and a delight to see them so happy. All

well worthwhile. Then someone sounded a discordant note. The parents didn't seem so elated. In fact many of them stood by with morose faces. After all the efforts, you would expect a little gratitude. Then a woman pointed out that maybe the parents were sad because they had to stand by and watch others give their children a gift for the fiesta. Ah yes, that was true. Obvious now that they thought of it. What parent wouldn't feel sad in those circumstances? Next time that they repeated this gesture, they would secretly pass the presents along to the parents and let them give them to their own offspring. All agreed this would be much better.

(3) Bible passage chosen: Amos 5: 21-24. A passage on justice that really shed light on the situation.

(4) Shared prayer (cf. Meeting 1, 3). The prayers were very related to the Bible reflections.

* * *

Meeting 21: Evaluation
The following are a list of questions that might help a small community to evaluate its life and action. The work can be spread over maybe three sessions, or a day (once a year?) be devoted to this rather complete assessment.

(1) The community places itself in the presence of God (silent pause).

(2) Check-in (cf. Meeting 4, 1).

(3) Bible reflection: Acts 15:1-35 (the apostles plan and evaluate). Does this passage shed any light on the evaluation exercise? Other possible readings to choose from should the task go to more than one session: Acts 6:1-7 (the apostles plan and evaluate); *Evangelica Testificatio (Evangelical Witness)*, Paul VI, no. 25 (cf.*Vatican Council II*, Flannery, Fifth Printing 1980, p. 692).

(4) Questions for evaluation exercise:

• Do we imitate the Blessed Trinity in our efforts to love and share?

• Is our community Christ-centred?

• Have we been able to maintain a relative autonomy from our mainstream Church while at the same time preserving links and a cooperative relationship?

• Is working for a society where there is goodness and harmony rooted in justice a priority for us?

- Have we made an option with the poor?
- Are women, youth, children and all who are disadvantaged and excluded given a voice and the opportunity to make their contribution?
- Are we open to others and prepared to change?
- Are we prepared to die like the grain of wheat?
- What are we growing into?
- Do we value the Eucharist, word of God, prayer, reconciliation and reflection?
- Is our use of the Bible life-related?
- Do we continually reflect on what we do and act on our reflection?
- Are our decisions truly arrived at through dialogue and consensus?
- Do we face up to and resolve conflict?

(5) What *action(s)* are to be taken as a result of the evaluation? (no more than four or five)

(6) Shared prayer (cf. Meeting 1, 3).

* * *

Meeting 22: Exercise/Group Dynamic

Theme: Self-confidence

This session is taken from notes that I made of an encounter in our Dublin community. It is probably better suited to a youthful group.

(1) Check-in (cf. Meeting 4, 1)

(2) There were musical chairs to enliven the proceedings. I hasten to add that the participants were young on the whole, so there were no sprained ankles.

(3) Soap-box activity: each member was seated on a central chair in turn and asked to speak spontaneously on a topic that was picked out of a hat. There were such items as: sliced bread, socks, ashtray, orange, curtains, giraffe. The group proved quite inventive and articulate in addressing these topics. The animator pointed out that the subjects were trivial and caused a lot of mirth. However, if people could speak on these they could speak on anything. Another member observed that it was good to have been put on the spot, because spontaneity helps self-confidence.

(4) There followed a more thorough debriefing in which these items were noticed:

- the need for people to affirm one another,
- the importance of paying attention,
- how necessary it is to have a certain inner toughness and not be overly sensitive,
- the need to believe in oneself,
- and how important family and community are for all of us.

(5) A selection of mottoes were then read out. Each member was asked to reflect on them and select one that appealed to him. Here are some examples:

- Let us be grateful for every single moment of this wonderful day!
- An optimist is someone who takes the cold water thrown upon an idea, heats it with enthusiasm, and then uses the steam to push ahead.
- Help me, Lord, to remember that there isn't anything that can happen today that you and I can't handle.

(6) Bible Reflection: Matthew 6: 25-34.

This is the beautiful passage that tells us how God looks after the birds of the air and the flowers of the field. Much more so, then, will that God look after all of us. And there in a nutshell is the ultimate reason why we face the ups and downs of life with self-confidence. Motivated by this thought, the members of the community determined to bring a sense of self-confidence to everything they did.

(7) The facilitator played a recording of Julie Andrew's animated version of 'I Have Confidence' from *The Sound of Music*.

(8) Shared prayer (cf. Meeting 1, 3). At the end all hold hands and recite the Lord's Prayer.

Memorable Sessions

A couple of meetings that I experienced in the course of my travels so impressed me that I wrote about them. I think it may prove helpful to quote them here. The first comes from West Africa:

Fr Emiliano and myself bumped along the deeply rutted dirt road in a jeep through the African bush. It was night. Occasionally the headlights would pick out the bejewelled eyes of some creature in the undergrowth, transfixed by the lights. We came to a halt near a cluster of huts. Emiliano got out and started to walk through the darkness. I followed in his wake, fearful that a snake might be slithering around at my feet. It's best to carry a lamp.

We entered a grass-roofed hut made of slats that was dimly lit by a storm lantern hanging from one corner. A small Christian community was assembled for its weekly meeting, the children seated on the floor in the middle and the adults on forms round the sides.

We were welcomed somewhat formally and the meeting began with a lively hymn to the accompaniment of drums. This was followed by a reading from Matthew 25 ('I was hungry and you fed me, thirsty and you gave me a drink etc.,). The members of the community then shared their insights on the passage; the exchange was truly impressive. The sharing over, the surrounding bush again echoed to the sound of enthusiastic singing and drumming that are features of African communities.

Then the crunch came. What were they going to do about the word of God which they had heard? Actually it emerged that they were already doing their bit. River blindness is a hazard in Sierra Leone, the country in question. People go searching for diamonds in the sediment of rivers and are bitten by a tiny organism in the waters. As a result they go blind unless treated, so, not surprisingly, Sierra Leone seems to have more blind people than usual. This small Christian community was taking care of some such persons and one of them was actually present at the meeting. They felt, therefore, that they were trying to do something about the word of God which they had heard, but decided to look more diligently to see if there were other folk, not necessarily blind, who might be in need of support.

More drumming and singing and then a call for prayer.

Heads bowed reverently. There was profound silence. A mosquito whirred at my ear and I became aware of the chafing of cicadas in the surrounding bush. The prayers began to flow freely from individuals at various points of the assembly. Moving prayers. Heartfelt prayers.

There was a boisterous final hymn followed by warm farewells as people melted away to their huts in the darkness. A young boy led the blind man by the hand. He lived in a world of darkness that was nevertheless filled with much light.

One of the things that impressed me about this meeting was the local flavouring of it all: the singing, the drumming, the setting, the issues, and so forth. It was so different and yet had much in common with meetings elsewhere.

* * *

The second encounter took place in Perth, Australia. My short account went like this:

There was a significant session in the house of Peter and Marya Stewart in Perth. Having tried to play a little football with a group of lively children, I went into the house to get my thoughts together for the Eucharist. The participation was striking. There were about 10 adults (parents) and 20 children present. What moved me was the involvement of the children. After the grown-ups had shared for some time on the gospel, someone asked: 'And what do the children think of the reading? Do they have anything to say?' *Did they have anything to say?* They had plenty to say and it made lots of sense.

During the Mass the children vied with one another to hold baby Eugene, who with great wondering eyes remained placid and hiccupping as he was passed around the assembly like snuff at a wake, as we say in Ireland. Those little ones who had not yet made their First Communion and, therefore, could not receive were given blessed bread, so that they didn't feel left out of the celebration.

Afterwards we shared a pot-luck meal. Care was taken to feed the young ones first. Then a video was put on for them and I got a chance to chat separately with the adults. These good people were interested in a wide variety of areas: peace and justice (the cause of the Aboriginals for example; next day I was to partake in a demonstration for Aboriginal land rights), liturgy, forms of community that would be a countersign to a materialistic and harshly secular world, how best to relate to the traditional Church, and youth of course.

Now and again a little one would stray in and sit on the lap of mummy or daddy, or lie down at their feet, be covered with a blanket, and fall asleep. The accommodation of the children, some of whom were in fact young teenagers, was beautiful to behold. Can the reader think of a better way of introducing

Christ and the gospel message to these children? I'm sure this small community, or family Church, will serve as a beacon throughout their whole lives.

Summary

(1) The essential components of the small Christian community meeting are: bonding, contemplation, and reality.
(2) The session ought to be relevant and flexible.
(3) As well as meetings proper, social encounters are effective means of building relationships.
(4) Some 22 examples of meetings are given, employing the following categories: exercise (group dynamic), worship, commitment, ecumenical, prophetic, planning, evaluation, commonly-used format, and miscellaneous.
(5) The themes embraced are: community, sharing, unity, word of God, prayer, Eucharist, reconciliation, commitment, kingdom of God, leadership, ecumenism, justice, environment, planning, evaluation, self-confidence.

Question

How does what has been said in this chapter relate to what happens in your own small Christian community?
Suggested Bible passage: John 4: 1-30 (Jesus' encounter with the Samaritan Woman). What do the participants in this meeting teach us, including the apostles who come in on the end of it?

CHAPTER 4

Pastoral Planning

I once heard a lay person plead for an end to drift and the making of a plan in this fashion: 'Fr A comes to our parish and does a lot of building. Then comes Fr B saying the people are the Church, not bricks and mortar, and gets groups going. Comes Fr C and he believes that, if you get the liturgy right, everything else will automatically follow.The result is that we, the laity, are completely bewildered. Is there no way that the diocese could have a plan, so that all the priests are concentrating on the same things?'

The situation described is not uncommon, and it is a bad situation. Indeed it is not just bad but completely counter-productive, because through lack of follow-up each pastor is undoing what his predecessor did.

Difficult though it undoubtedly is in a world where all is sand shifting beneath our feet, we must nevertheless strive to plan. As already noted, a small Christian community ought to have a plan of action from the outset that will respond to some obvious needs round about. There might, for example, be a lot of elderly and house-bound people in a district who would welcome a frequent visit. But as a community grows in maturity, it could feel the need of making a thoroughgoing pastoral plan for its area. This entails understanding the religious, political, social, and economic realities of a situation as seen by the ordinary people of the locality. To do this the group needs to make a careful study of the situation. I shall outline a method that has been honed through practice and which, I believe, can be adapted to wider situations.

The planning method in question has eight steps that are fairly common to most planning procedures. All of them are of importance to the process, so there should be no shortcuts. *The process involved is just as important in terms of the resulting benefits as the plan itself, so it absolutely should not be rushed.* Depending on the size of the area, difficulty or ease of communication, we are talking of months, even a year or two. A far-flung province of my order spent three years making a plan. But, believe me, it really was far-flung. The steps involved are as follows:

(1) The planning team positions itself.
(2) The approach.
(3) First meeting at grassroots.
(4) Second meeting at grassroots.
(5) Examination of problems/issues.
(6) Analysis of systems.
(7) An overall view.
(8) Practical outcome or planning.

(1) The team positions itself

The team, most of whom will be chosen from the small Christian community which will accompany them all the way in the task, must interest themselves in the total environment. If the group contains some persons qualified in relevant disciplines so much the better. Ordinarily, however, this is not possible, in which case the team chosen will equip themselves through the practical experience of doing the task. The appropriate disciplines would be theology, catechetics, psychology, sociology, anthropology, and economics.

To begin immersing themselves in the total environment, the team carries out a preliminary survey with instructions and questions that are crystal clear. Such clarity in queries and instructions must characterize the whole planning process. This survey should assist them in getting to know the place better as regards:

• climate;
• boundaries, mountains, hills, ravines (physical features);
• rivers, canals, lakes, and sea (waterways);
• roads, rail, electricity, gas, water supply, and sewage (infrastructure);
• buses, trains, and taxis (transport);
• post, telephone system, newspapers, radio, television, computers (social communications);
• living conditions, ethnic groups, customs, hospitals, schools, cinemas, and places of assembly (social, cultural, and educational factors).

The results of this preliminary survey are then written up and, if necessary, a map is drawn.

The team is engaged in *pastoral planning* and not in a merely social operation. The first step, therefore, and every phase of the planning process, will be done in the light of the word of God, prayer, and Church documents. And the same will be true of the subsequent implementation.

(2) The approach

Despite the initial contact made in the foregoing phase, the planning team and small community may not be fully in touch with their people. They must do something to remedy this. In the first phase they will have come closer to some of the ordinary inhabitants of the area, so they can commence conversing with them on a variety of matters including these:

- the family,
- position of women,
- situation of youth,
- treatment of children,
- working conditions,
- rate of unemployment,
- cultural events,
- main sicknesses,
- political involvement, and
- religious practices.

From these conversations the team will draw up *a first version of a list of problems.* They must, however, realize that this initial approach will not produce a profound knowledge of the area.

There is a tendency of which the team must be aware from the start. It is a strong inclination on their part to colour all the findings with their own way of thinking. In short it becomes a matter of the problems *as they see them* and not as the people generally see them. There has to be a major effort to eliminate this weakness. So folk must be thoroughly consulted.

(3) First meeting at grassroots

It is precisely to involve fellow-residents and delve deeper into the reality of the place that a first meeting at grassroots is held. The participants at this meeting will be the planning team, the members of the small community, and the persons whom the team have come closer to in the previous stages.

At the meeting those taking part should be presented with the first version of a list of problems, which was worked out in the second step, and asked to think carefully about it. They may *add to* or *modify* the list as they think fit.

The organizers of the meeting have to get beyond the point where the people may be telling them what they think they want to hear – another great pitfall in pastoral planning. This can only be done through establishing trust through patient, prolonged dialogue. It is therefore important to allow adequate time for this. I recall taking part in this first meeting at grassroots in a South American *barrio*. It seemed at the outset that the greatest worry of the people was to provide a steeple for the church – in an area where there was poverty, malnutrition, astronomical unemployment, lack of formal education, drugs, drunkenness, and prostitution. Lengthy dialogue showed that the steeple was among the least of their felt needs, and 23 years later the church is still without one.

This meeting ought to provide *a second more authentic list of problems*.

Incidentally, though this method is based on dialogue, the team may find it convenient here or at other points of the planning process to allow written submissions. These can be anonymous. This might prove helpful to certain shy individuals; personal attacks, however, and outlandish statements, unhelpful to the procedure, ought to be discarded.

(4) Second meeting at grassroots

Up to this point the organizing team, even without knowing it, may be unduly influencing proceedings. So they must try anew to eliminate any possible bias from the proceedings.

Furthermore, people may be somewhat reticent of each other and of the team. Time is needed so that all concerned get to know each other better.

To solve such difficulties as these, a second meeting at grassroots is held. The number of participants is greatly increased from the previous meeting. After a brief introduction and, perhaps, a dynamic to relate people, they are presented with *the second version of a list of problems*. Then they are divided into convenient groups and urged to think carefully about the list and make relevant comments.

The planning team must be satisfied that there are a sufficient number of persons present to make the gathering authentic. Sixty, representing a good cross-section of the residents, would seem a desirable attendance. If there aren't that many present, a repeat supplementary session could be held to ensure that a sufficient body of people are consulted.

Following the group meetings a general session is held to pool ideas.

This encounter should root out most of the defects of the second list of problems and lead to a meeting of minds. Items may be dropped, added to, or altered. In short the team will likely discover a much more valid catalogue of issues.This will represent *the third and final list*.

And this is also the point in the planning process where we try to identify the generative problems on our list. *By generative problems we mean those that give birth to many others*. Abject poverty , for example, can lead to hunger, disease, crime, prostitution, and so on.

(5) Examination of problems

Equipped with the third and finalized list of problems and perhaps even more importantly with a list of generative problems, the team must now move on to a more profound examination of the situation. Even if they have been proceeding in the planning process without professional help, they would do well to bring in some qualified person(s) at this particular stage. But again, only if it is possible.

So far the team has been dealing with the problems as they show themselves outwardly. Indeed, they have been striving to make sense of a most complicated reality. Now they must face an even greater challenge and endeavour to examine the *root causes* of the problems under consideration. This the team does with the help of the remaining members of the small community and some of their acquaintances from the district.

There is a number of questions that need answering, such as these:

- Is the problem new?
- If not, how far back does it go?
- Why wasn't something done about it long before?
- Has the make-up of the people (attitudes, how they see the world, their manner of thinking) anything to do with the problem?
- Can't the authorities, the law; or anybody remedy the situation?
- What can the participants in the meeting and people like them do about a solution?
- Do they need to organize?

These questions should help to winkle out relevant historical, religious, social, psychological, cultural, and economic factors that are at work in the situation.

(6) Analysis of systems

The previous stage leads naturally to a consideration of how the society in which we live is organized. This can bring the participants face to face with oppressive structures which cry out for 'bold transformations and innovations that go deep.'[1] For nearly three decades now the Church has been insisting that we must look to the very structures of our society and do something about those. A dab of paint here or a nail there is not enough. Unjust structures divide people into haves and have-nots, included and excluded, and condemn millions to real death or a living death through misery, hunger, and disease.

And oppressive structures give rise to values, attitudes, and actions that are widespread and utterly blighted by selfishness. To deal effectively with these we must get at the causes.

(7) An overall view

As the team and its associates analyze systems, they inevitably find that the problems they encounter are widespread. They may have differing aspects from area to area, but basically they are the same. The evils found in the locality under consideration are to be found in neighbouring areas, in the province, nation, continent, and indeed in the whole world.

East and West, North and South ordinary persons are the victims of powerful structures preserved by elites who inculcate false values, who gain profit at the expense of people, power at the expense of people. In this, unfortunately, they are often aided and abetted by the media and corrupt politicians. But the great mass of humanity founder in misery and powerlessness. One of the great causes of our time is that of the dispossessed of the earth, and not to involve ourselves is to remain on the margins of history.

(8) Planning

When we come to planning, or what we are going to do in practice, we must look hard at root causes and generative problems and strike at these. It is best to be specific here. Let us return to the South American *barrio*, or poor urban district, that I mentioned above in stage 2. Remember its appalling list of problems? Grinding poverty, malnutrition, astronomical unemployment, illiteracy, lack of formal education, crime, drugs, drunkenness, prostitution, and so forth. When we came to getting to the root causes of these issues, we came to the following conclusions:

- *Oppression and marginalization* at the hands of the wealthy and powerful elite who ran the country, in league with multi-national corporations and foreign banks, were the main factors that blighted the lives of residents in the *barrio*. They engendered *a poor self-image* among the people, *deprived them of culture and a formal education*, sank them in *poverty*, and caused *disunity*, because the oppressor could easily sow division among them.
- There is a perversity that is to be found together with good in the heart of every human being, even in that of the oppressed, and this too has to be taken into account and combatted. It prevents people from uniting for their own good.

To deal with these we took the following course:

Solution

This would be provided by a liberating:
- evangelization,
- conscientization,
- education, and
- social action.

By the term *liberating* we meant that the solution would come largely from the person herself in interaction with others.

Activities

Evangelization or passing on the faith
(with a view to enriching folk spiritually and improving the moral
climate):
- youth ferment group,
- seven small Christian communities,
- courses,
- retreats,
- youth Mass,
- youth Easter,
- bringing gospel/human values to the home, neighbourhood,
  spheres of work, study, business, and leisure, and
- five catechetical centres, each with an attached children's club.

Conscientization /Social Action
(Conscientization is the awareness which comes from continually
reflecting upon the issues of life and acting on that reflection so as
to change the world):
- *barrio* magazine,
- notice boards,
- posters,
- meetings,
- conferences, and
- discussions.

Education/Social Action
- literacy,
- accountancy,
- cooking and hygiene,
- dress-making,
- commercial crafts' centre,
- first aid,
- electrical installation,
- guitar,
- English,
- individual tutoring, and
- a night school for people who had missed out on education and
  others who wanted it.

When it came to action, we could only work with the resources we had and, as we said, bring them to bear on the above evils. We didn't have vast sums of money. What we did have was a good number of enthusiastic young people willing to help their *barrio* and this is reflected in the above plan of action. The area was in fact teeming with young folk and their well-being was a major concern. Twenty or more years later the place has lost its former notoriety and progressed greatly. I feel sure that the above effort played some part in this happy outcome. But there was always a solid core of some of the finest people I have ever met in that area. At the time of planning the district was bearing the brunt of migration as landless *campesinos* flocked into the city from the rural areas, signalling a dire need for land reform.

In chapter 2 on organization we mentioned how small Christian communities have agreed principles, values, understandings and commitments. They would have had these long before setting out on the pastoral plan. Indeed sometimes the communities have four or five broad-based statements, or a Rule of Life, that express their aspirations for building the kingdom of God. Following the planning, they must now examine their Rule, whether it be implicit or explicit, to see how it squares up with the new scheme of things. The two together then provide a pathway into the future.

In going through the above exercise, we are following in the footsteps of the early Christians. During painful and confused times they looked at the reality of their lives in the light of Christ and forged paths into an uncertain future. I have no inclination to gaze into a crystal ball to make predictions about the future Church in this precipitously changing world of ours. But I feel confident that the seeds of the Church of the future are already here in the present and that the Holy Spirit will help us to discern them. And we can move forward from there.

Implementation and evaluation

A pastoral plan must not just remain on paper; it has to be resolutely implemented. It also has to be evaluated periodically from all aspects: spiritual, intellectual, intuitive, human, and practical. Adjustments are made when required. The small community will do these things, yet everything should not be made to fall upon them. The eventual success of the endeavour will depend on the continued involvement of those whom it touches. All must own it. All must take responsibility for it. This list of questions may facilitate the work of evaluation:

- Are we making a persevering attempt as individuals and as a community to implement the plan?
- If not, why not?
- Do we need to make adjustments?
- Has there been progress?
- Have we sought to involve the people of our area, especially all those consulted in the making of the plan?
- Are we united and organized?
- Do we respect process, yet have a sense of urgency?
- Are our endeavours to implement the pastoral plan backed by a profound spirituality?

Implementation is of course the acid test. 'To make a ragout you must first catch your hare.' So said one Doctor Hill in a work entitled *Cook Book* (1747)[2] – at least the volume was attributed to him. One can imagine old Doctor Hill chuckling to himself as, tongue in cheek, he saw the double meaning in what he had written. Now, making a pastoral plan is one thing; implementing it quite another. Implementing it is the pastoral equivalent of catching your hare. I hope the foregoing questions may help people to do so. But where hares are concerned, I prefer my hares running wild and free, thank you, Dr Hill.

Summary

(a) A small community would do well to have a plan of action that responds to obvious needs.
(b) As a group grows in maturity it might feel a need to make a thoroughgoing pastoral plan for its area.
(c) This is a demanding undertaking, involving an analysis of the religious, political, social, and psychological realities of the district as the residents see them.
(d) The community selects a team to spearhead the endeavour, and then the following steps are employed:
    (1) The planning team positions itself.
    (2) The approach.

(3) First meeting at grassroots.

(4) Second meeting at grassroots.

(5) Examination of problems/issues.

(6) Analysis of systems.

(7) An overall view.

(8) Planning.

(These steps are dealt with succinctly in the text.)

(e) The group resolutely implements, and periodically evaluates (questions provided) the plan.

(f) Ideally all the people of the district will somehow be involved with the plan.

Question

Does your small Christian community or group have, or feel the need for, a plan?

Suggested Bible passage: Luke 10: 1-20.

Does this passage provoke any thoughts on the matter of planning?

CHAPTER 5

Common Issues

Owing to the nature of this book, we are of course touching on practical issues all the way through. However, there are some items which I feel we ought to single out for special treatment, and I shall now do so.

Diversity

Having completed a workshop in an Australian town, I returned with a sister who had organized the session to the bishop's house. As I went upstairs, I couldn't help but overhear the bishop say to the sister down below in a rather resigned voice, 'Well, what's the *word* this time?' To which the sister replied resoundingly, 'Flexibility.' Heaving a great sigh of relief, the bishop declared, 'Thanks be to God!'

There is no *blueprint* for the establishment of small communities, *no one methodology, no one structure and no one way.* So we must be open to diversity and allow for flexibility. If there is a method that helps me, well and good, but I cannot presume that it has to be the path for everyone. I always insist myself that I haven't got a neat package tied up in ribbons to deliver, *only insights and guidelines drawn from experience to share.* Insights and guidelines many of which I have learned from others in the field. I ask participants in workshops to look at these *in the light of their own experience* to see if there is anything that might be of help to them. The groups respond to, and are fashioned greatly by, the environment in which they find themselves. So it would be a considerable mistake to try and plant a Chilean model in Australia, or indeed a Rockhampton model in neighbouring Townsville. This whole phenomenon of small community is only in its infancy in the modern era. It is not a time to be setting things in concrete. We have to be ready to sit humbly at the feet of experience and learn.

There is a desire in many human beings, particularly in the affluent world, to tie up loose ends. We find it extremely hard to live with
the mess that being a member of our Church often entails. We grasp
at a particular structure or methodology as if it were a security blanket, stoutly refusing to entertain other possibilities. But what is the
point of replacing one model of Church that we regard as hide-
bound with another that is equally so?

As I said elsewhere, I do realize that people may need something solid to hang on to at the beginning; very often they may be
coming out of a situation where the Church is highly institutional-
ized. With time, however, flexibility should appear. Very often the
people, guided no doubt by the Spirit who is a great one for turning
the world upside-down, make their own communities more mal-
leable.

Let me return once more to the constants of the groups, or those
elements embraced by the terms:

- bonding.
- contemplation, and
- reality.

These ought to be factors in the life of every small Christian community in the world. They are the transcultural essentials. But once
these vital ingredients are present, varying structure, method, and
style should then grow most naturally from the native soil. There
has to be the homespun Ballyjamesduff version.

Apart from diversity within the groups, there is diversity all
around us. In the Church we have progressives and conservatives,
people who are advocates of a Vatican II model and those who
hearken back to the pre-Vatican way; there are the active and the
passive, those who are within and a growing number who are
alienated. Most are trying to make some sense of their Church and
their lives. Oftentimes the debate between disparate elements has
been high-pitched and acrimonious. Intolerance has reared its ugly
head. It is now time to turn down the volume, respect one another,
listen carefully to each other, and strive to dialogue even with folk
in the most extreme positions. There is no other way forward. We
badly need the good Samaritans who will pour the balm of healing
oil on our wounds and divisions.

For centuries we have had uniformity in the Church. No more.
Approaching the third millennium we must learn to live with

diversity, yet always speak our truth, and always be ready to challenge and be challenged. In short we have to learn to live and let live, never forgetting the words of St Paul: 'Let all be done in love' (1 Corinthians 16:14).

Liturgy is most important to us, and an example taken from that area could help. In a South American parish, where I worked, a youth Mass was put on at an appropriate time on Sunday evenings. There were guitars and lively hymns and the young people were as plentiful as potatoes, as they say in that part of the world. The whole thing was a heartening success.

But after one such celebration a lady came to me full of indignation. She didn't like guitars. The singing was raucous (it was!) and there was quite a lot of talking. In short she felt she hadn't been to Mass at all. This had to stop. I felt upset. However, a little voice in my head said, 'Now just a moment ...' Anyway, I went on to point out quietly to her that this was a celebration for young people, and whatever about our own personal tastes we had to meet the needs of those teenagers. At least they were now coming to church which wasn't the case before. And as for the singing, sometimes we have to listen to the music of the young with the heart and not with the ears. Also, in the parish there were a few other Masses of a subdued nature provided for persons like herself who preferred that style. She calmed down somewhat and I heard no more about it. The liturgy is a good example of a situation in which we have to be tolerant of, and cater for, diversity.

Finally, if we can cope with disparity in our own house, then we will have some hope of coping with the wide world out there characterized by an enormous variety of race, creed, and practice. Many people feel threatened by what is different in terms of ethnic origin, religion, or colour. Jesus on the contrary rejoiced in difference. The kingdom of God is like a great net, he tells us, that gathers all manner of fish (cf. Matthew 13:47). There is ample room for everyone.

I find that parable of the net intriguing. While in Australia I had occasion to visit the Great Barrier Reef Museum in Townsville, Queensland. My mind simply boggled at the numerous types of fish of every conceivable shape, size, and colour swimming about among the gloriously blooming coral. Some had beetling brows reminding one somehow of Socrates; others had a predatory look, still others a busy eager-beaver mien. As I gazed on their infinite variations, the thought came to me that our Creator just loves diversity.

Ecumenism

Closely related to the issue of diversity is that of ecumenism. It is urgent. One of the most heartfelt prayers of Christ coming towards the end of his life was:

> ... that they may all be one;
> even as thou, Father, art in me,
> and I in thee...' (John 17:21).

So the question is never whether we shall or shall not do something about ecumenism. The only question is what exactly are we going to do? What is the best course in our situation? A Church is Christian insofar as it is ecumenical.

Where small Christian communities are concerned, we can identify two possibilities. There can be groups belonging to particular denominations and those composed of members from various denominations. Both are necessary. The inter-denominational, or ecumenical, ones of course give a very powerful witness to unity and as such must be promoted and encouraged. In order that this should work, I believe it is important for the persons who compose an inter-denominational community to be sure of their own identity. They have to respect one another's beliefs and not set out to proselytize each other. In short it requires a fair degree of Christian maturity. If we get confused Catholics coming together with confused Protestants, great could be the confusion thereof.

Even where small communities are denominational, they are still ecumenical. Our Dublin group, although situated in an area that is almost totally Roman Catholic, is nevertheless very ecumenically minded. We have tried to link up with the local Church of Ireland community, attended the meetings of inter-denominational groups, invited people of other denominations, even other religions, to come and chat and pray with us. We have been in demonstrations of different kinds with members of various denominations and indeed of none. This year we were joined by Olive who has recently been ordained a priest in the Church of Ireland. Her cheerful presence enriched our community enormously. The community, though mature, is youthful on the whole and seems to have no trouble with being marvellously open.

We have just noticed how people of disparate denominations
get together to demonstrate for worthy causes. This is a level of
commingling that should present no problem. To sink a well, build
a hospital, or struggle to have prisoners-of-conscience released, are
matters on which we can all get together.

Regarding ecumenism, I have found Africa of great interest.
Over most of that vast continent it doesn't present the problems
that it does elsewhere in the world, because even within extended
families you have members of varying denominations. I heard a
bishop tell of how in his extended family there were Roman
Catholics, Anglicans, and Pentecostals. It really depended on the
school they attended as children. Yet they all lived together in harmony; as the bishop so rightly said, 'We can't *afford* to do otherwise.'

An African Cardinal once told Pope John Paul, who marvelled
at the story, that his father had been a chief who professed the
native religion and had eight wives. Indeed depending on where
one lived in Africa, he could have family members belonging to, not
simply other Christian denominations, but different religions as
well. Relating to fellow Christians, therefore, is hardly an issue at
all. I have a friend, Joachim, who is going on to be a Catholic priest,
whereas his sister is studying to be a Pentecostal pastor. They both
deeply love and respect each other, and the mother said, 'I am
happy because you are both doing something good.' The Africans,
fortunately, do not trail our historical baggage where ecumenism is
concerned. Are they not perhaps saying to us that the eventual
unity of all Christians will be a *unity in diversity*?

Members of different religions, Christian and Muslim for example, relate easily and work together. Again they can be from the
same extended family so how could it sensibly be otherwise? Fr
Tony in Sierra Leone was celebrating the Eucharist on the occasion
of the harvest festival in a small village. The church was packed
largely with Muslims. Before the ceremony was finished, the
muezzin in the tower of the nearby mosque started calling all his co-
religionists for prayer, because it was a Friday. Nobody stirred in
the church. All reverently remained until the Mass concluded. Then
they trooped off faithfully to the mosque. I have been at Christian
funerals where the great majority of those praying for the soul of
the departed have been Muslims; the Christians would have the

same openness. Here surely is a sign of great hope for the Church and the world.

Residential Small Christian Communities

We find yet another manifestation of unity in diversity when disparate elements come together to make communities, such as, different families or laity and religious. There is a difficulty involved here, but, before we deal with it, let us just note that, when we enter a residential community, it is a much more intense experience than being part of a neighbourhood group. That is not to say that one form is better than the other; simply that they are different calls. However, there are persons who will want, and indeed even need, to go the road of residential community no matter what. If one is in doubt, it might be best to test the waters in a non-residential set-up for a start.

In South Africa (to return to our original point) I found three families who joined together in a big rambling house to make a residential community. I asked the teenage daughter of one of them how she felt about the project. She told me how at first she strongly opposed the whole idea, but was persuaded by her parents to give it a try. She did so and was totally won over to the experiment. Her fear at the beginning was that she would lose her family – that their identity would be lost in the melting pot. However, the group sensibly left space for family life; there were the times when the families were alone for sharing meals, prayer, and life and the times when they joined the others. It worked. The key to success being that space was made for the individual families. To do this, of course, there also has to be the physical room.

The same would, I believe, prove true for laity and religious coming together. They would have to be respectful of, and make space for, the different identities.

Small Christian communities and the traditional Church

By and large small Christian communities have operated within their mainstream Churches. They have existed in the margins at times and there may have been tensions between them and the official body. Still they persevered. I think the position of my own community regarding the local parish would be fairly typical of many groups in countries where the Church is long established. Our relationship with it is good. We worship there, have a member on the pastoral council, and others performing different ministries.The parish lets us be; no opposition on the one hand, but no great involvement on the other. I could say that we are in the margins. That is because ours is one model of Church, the communitarian, while the parish would be in the traditional, pyramidal mode. Many of the parishioners would in fact be of an advanced age; so it is the model that places us in the margins rather than any form of acrimony.

On the other hand many small communities are being fostered by the mainstream Church. This is particularly so in economically deprived countries, but not only there as we shall remember from our historical profile. Throughout the world there are whole parishes and dioceses that have opted for the community model. Africa, for example, has made a commitment to Family Church at its recent Synod. We mentioned the circumstances that made the choice inevitable. As a West African bishop put it, 'For us it's the only way.'

We already alluded to the debate as to whether the seeds of the future Church are in the mainstream or in the margins. What I have seen myself leads me to believe that both will play their part.

More than once we have referred to the need for networking; the value of linking groups together so that they get the experience of being a *communion of communities*. How might this come about? Where groups are numerous, it makes the task easier. I have seen parishes, even dioceses, where communities come together for meetings and celebrations. Take the case of our Dublin community. There are only a few groups in our parish, so we are reaching out beyond its boundaries in an effort to do this. It makes one wonder if our present system of parishes and dioceses, with their rigid demarcation lines, will survive in a world that is becoming ever more mobile and person-centred. *Community* more than *geography* will surely be the key; areas will probably be reference points, but with soft margins. And they will be secondary to people and their needs. Even in the contemporary Church, because of the diversity that we referred to above, there are people who cross parish limits to satisfy their spiritual requirements. Ideally, we should have the *oikos*, or house Church, and beyond that a centre which would serve as a sort of staging-post for neighbourhood groups – be a place where they could be refreshed and motivated. It would not, of course, be all one-way traffic, because the centre would also be greatly enriched by the small communities.

There are those who foresee the demise of the *parish* and the *diocese.* Presumably they are speaking of the model in which they now operate, because, call them what you will, we are going to need those more enlarged entities where we can get the crucial experience of being *a communion of communities.*

Inculturation

This is a word that is much bandied about these days. Its content is to be found in the words of the Gospel of John: 'And the Word became flesh and dwelt among us…' (John 1:14). The gospel *has to be made flesh and blood* in the lives and circumstances of those to whom it is preached, and this is a complex procedure that doesn't happen overnight, as the *Working Paper for the African Synod*, no. 49 reminds us:

> The process of the Church's insertion into people's cultures is a lengthy one. It is not a matter of purely external adaptation, for inculturation means the intimate transformation of authentic cultural values through their integration in Christianity and the insertion of Christianity into the various human cultures.[1]

Christianity then is profoundly affected by the human culture and the human culture by Christianity. There is a double effect.

It may not always be a soothing effect. A religious provincial was once visiting a community of his province. A great wall topped with broken glass surrounded the building where they lived. The provincial wondered if the glass was there to keep the thieves out or the religious in, to which one wag replied, 'I suppose it cuts both ways, Father.'

Well, the gospel is a two-edged sword. What is good in our cultures it affirms; what is not good it challenges. Too easily we can appeal to culture to give the stamp of approval to something defective. Here in Ireland we have a delicate peace process. It has come after twenty-five years of violence during which Christians killed Christians. Muslims and Christians are still embroiled in the Balkan tragedy; all worship the one God. And there was the Rwandan catastrophe that shook Africa to its core. Really, as we approach the year 2000, the Churches must seriously question themselves as to whether or not they are reaching down and *challenging cultures at depth*. Paul was adamant with the sexually promiscuous Corinthians. They could not do those heinous deeds and still call themselves followers of Christ. No pussy-footing there. Nor does Jesus tread lightly when he declares:

> You have heard
> that it was said to those of ancient times,
> 'You shall not murder';
> and 'whoever murders shall be liable to judgment.'
> But I say to you
> that if you are angry with a brother or sister,
> you will be liable to judgment;
> and if you insult a brother or sister,
> you will be liable to the council;
> and if you say, 'You fool,'
> you will be liable to the hell of fire.
> (Matthew 5: 21-22)

If the Churches were as determined as Jesus and Paul in announcing the good news, it would offer enormous hope as we enter the third millennium.

When the problem of inculturation is discussed, usually it is connected with the missions in places like Africa and Asia. What we can forget is that the issue exists for all cultures. More so today than ever. In a world of headlong change, cultures change too, and every generation has to receive the faith afresh. Culture is often associated with folklore and tradition; however, it is also *the living and altering present* and not simply the past. The word has to be made flesh in the here and now.

And there is the further complication nowadays that youth have their own culture and can only be reached in and through it. A parish I know put on a Mass for young people. The pastor insisted that they come properly dressed and with hair neatly combed. The celebration was poorly attended. The youth in fact went in good numbers to another parish where they could come with sunglasses, designer holes in the knees of their jeans, and hair untamed. Simon the Zealot probably looked something like that. We must try to understand and address the current culture of young people and, obviously, there will be aspects of it that go much deeper than dress or appearance. For example, their reluctance to commit themselves in a rapidly changing, wildly uncertain, and frequently dangerous world.

Music is the language of the youth culture; it speaks to the soul of teenagers more than any other medium. I once saw this ever so lengthy queue on a Dublin street; all waiting to buy U2's latest album. And I asked myself if we are really using music enough to communicate Christ and his message.

And there is the hunger for peace and justice which many young people have, and a tender concern for the environment ... We could go on. There are also the darker aspects that need challenging of course; drink and drugs for instance. As I write, I am conscious that eight youth in our area of Dublin have died from drugs within a short period. What a terrible waste of young lives.

While we strive to know and respect a different culture to the best of our ability, we can never fully enter into it. I can never be a Masai and, if I were to don their national costume, I'm quite sure it would cause them no little amusement.

And what of the basic Christian community in the context of inculturation? It is the privileged place in which inculturation can happen and a powerful unit for promoting it. The groups are indeed *indispensable instruments of inculturation*. This, I realize, is quite a claim and I hope it will be justified when we come to share something of the theological vision. Just to mention liturgy as an example; we cannot supply a recipe for the whole world; only the communities can bring it alive in their own situations.

Youth

What of youth and the small communities? Clearly, since the groups are truly cells of the Church, they must be open to everyone; and the Church accommodates and involves persons of all ages. Not surprisingly then we find youthful people in the communities throughout the world; oftentimes in the role of coordinator. This is as it should be. Having said this, however, there are considerable cultural difficulties in the way of their involvement is some places. In Africa, especially in the rural areas, youth tend to be somewhat muted in the presence of adults. As you can imagine this puts a considerable block in the way of their meaningful participation. To solve this problem the youth in certain parts are forming their own Christian groups, run along the same lines as the small Christian communities, to parallel the adult gatherings. Still they look for occasions to come together for celebrations and sharing of experiences. In this way they hope with time to erode barriers. We might mention again that people having groups of their own for strong cultural reasons is a possibility, provided they *remain open* to other communities and groupings.

Africa is not standing still. Like the rest of the planet it too is changing. In the cities you can find the youth fitting easily into meetings with adults and speaking readily. I was at a gathering of groups in Nairobi a few years ago and a young man stood up and spoke out quite boldly and eloquently. Later one of the elders congratulated him for his courage and for having spoken so well. In years gone by he might have thought that this young upstart was getting too big for his boots.

Where young folk are concerned, there is another factor that has to be reckoned with nowadays. The reader will recall that, besides sharing the common culture of their ethnic groups, they have also developed their own youth culture whose spread owes much to the mass media. Naturally in communicating Christ to them one has to take account of this factor. This is why I think it is good for youth to have their own Christian groups to discuss issues of concern to them and to pray together, even where they can also be part of the adult communities.

In Zimbabwe recently I was giving a workshop in a distant mission that had no priest. There was a large and enthusiastic gathering, among them many teenagers who followed all most attentively. When there was group work, the young folk all got together and had the most animated discussions. I felt boundless admiration for them, because they were keeping this group going themselves and were excited by some ideas they had picked up in the sessions. They were determined to try and do something about them. I really felt the presence of the Spirit among them and the words of the psalm came to me: *I myself will shepherd them* (cf. Isaiah 40:9-11; Matthew 11:28).

Another heartening aspect of the episode was that right before my eyes, by the power of the Holy Spirit, I could see being realized the dream of Vatican II when it says:

The young should become the first apostles of the young, in direct contact with them, exercising the apostolate by themselves among themselves, taking account of their social environment. (*Decree on the Apostolate of the Laity*, 12).

Women

Women form the backbone of small Christian communities around the globe. Yet in certain societies that are heavily dominated by males, they are not allowed to realize their full potential and rarely would you find them in leadership roles. This too is changing. In Africa I am now beginning to come across some women coordinators, and for the sake of the communities one would hope that this trend continues and grows. The gifts of warmth, intuition, understanding, empathy, and spirituality that women bring are the lifeblood of community.

Women's groups, such as the Mothers of St Anne, flourish in Africa. In such gatherings they get to discuss their common problems and support each other, and they hone the group skills which they need in mixed communities. There is, then, a real point to these gatherings.

The question is often raised as to why women are much more of a presence in small Christian communities than men. When the question is put to myself, there is a little routine I go through. I ask these questions. Who travelled with Jesus ministering to him during his public life? Who came forth willingly and wiped his face on the road to Calvary? Who wept over him on that same road? Who stood by the cross when all the apostles save John had fled? And who were the first witnesses to the Resurrection? The participants, especially the womenfolk, chime in with the appropriate responses. Then I put the final query: So what's new?

Regarding the original question, I might just point out that where small communities are vibrant *and life-related*, they seem to attract men and women equally.

The Eucharist

In various Christian denominations the Eucharist is important to the groups, which doesn't necessarily mean that they manage to have celebrations frequently. In our small community in Dublin we have a meaningful Eucharist together about once every three months. For the rest we go to our parish, if possible to the same Mass.

Sad to relate, though the Eucharist is so central for many Christians, there is a veritable Eucharistic famine in the world through a shortage of priests. Numerous communities – more than sixty per cent in fact – can go without the Eucharist for months, even years.[2] A man from the Ecuadorean Andes once told me that his people were lucky if they had Mass once every two years. Which tends to make pointless Christ's injunction: 'Do this in memory of me' (Luke 22:19).

This issue exercizes the mind of communities a great deal and they hazard possible solutions: recall laicized priests who wish to function, allow married and women priests; they even wonder if a lay person might not be allowed to preside in the absence of a priest. It is a vexed and complex question. For one thing the traditional office of bishop, priest, and deacon go back to the dawn of the Church's history. What is the significance of this? Another consideration would be that, if the number of priests were to increase dramatically in the Church as it is now constituted, it might have the unwelcome complication of reinforcing clericalism. Hardly desirable as the laity struggle even now to play their full part in affairs.

I believe that this problem of priestly vocations can only be resolved in the context of a renewed communitarian Church, as envisaged by Vatican II, and realized through small Christian communities. From these groups the ministries needed can emerge. How many communities have we not seen in remote villages and outstations that are served by some exemplary persons, many of them married, who are really pillars of the Church? Such people could be promoted and ordained. Communities in Latin America were beginning to produce their own vocations in the seventies and imaginative means were used to prepare them, but the approach was discouraged in favour of the traditional seminary. Maybe it is an idea whose time has now come. In recent decades the Bible was put back in the hands of the laity with telling effect. Now our problem is how to give the Eucharist back to the faithful.

The RCIA and Small Christian Communities

Many parishes in recent years have been enthused by the RCIA
Movement (Rite of Christian Initiation of Adults). However, the
enthusiasm oftentimes wanes, because people who have been
through the course somehow disappear off the scene and are no
longer to be found in the parish. This is deeply disappointing, yet, I
feel, very understandable. The participants usually have the experience of a wonderfully intimate year together and then at the end of
it they are thrown back into the cold pond of the old-time parish.
The shock to the system proves too much. So we are back to the
futility of renewing the wine without renewing the wineskin. The
RCIA will only fully succeed in a Church that is utterly transformed
by the vision of Vatican II.

Ideally, then, those who complete the RCIA programme should
have vibrant small Christian communities into which they can
merge. Better still, the initiation should take place in the small communities in the first place. After all, every Christian is part of a
learning process; it's simply that people are at different stages.

In a previous chapter I mentioned the case of the Dublin parish
which had all those praiseworthy committees to run its activities on
behalf of the disadvantaged of every kind. The extent of their work
became clear in the course of a seminar on small Christian communities. The parish priest, or pastor, was away for the early sessions.
On his return I was speaking with him and he informed me that
there was still one group in the area who needed support, namely,
young married women, and he felt that the small Christian community would be the ideal 'committee' to take up this task. I said nothing at the time. But in group work at the end of the course, the
parishioners made it quite clear that their understanding of small
Christian community was not that it was just one more committee
added on to the others, or a ready tool at father's disposal for any
activity he might deem fit. For them it was a whole new communitarian way of being Church. Concern for young marrieds might
well be part of their agenda, but then again, it might not. It was a
matter for discernment within the community and this process had
to be respected. The upshot of this for us priests is that we must be
sensitive to the dynamics of these groups and never impose ourselves upon them.

We might mention in passing that the small communities are sometimes used as convenient units for parish fund-raising. Each member is asked to come up with a fixed sum – often not inconsiderable. I feel the community is not the place for this; it can frighten off poor people. Usually a group has a small fund for emergencies, which is administered by a team rather than by an individual. Faith-sharing is the priority; money is secondary. It should not be allowed to become the dominating problem it sometimes does.

Politics

Where does politics sit with the small Christian community? Politics is the dynamic way in which our whole secular life is organized; it concerns itself with health, labour, sport, finance, education, industry and commerce, communications, welfare, and so forth. That is why we have government ministries to look after all of these areas. Is the Church and its communities at the grassroots to have nothing to say about such matters? Must Christians busy themselves with incense and votive candles or retire to the sacristy? This is precisely what our opponents often understand by keeping out of politics. Of course this is absurd. We cannot opt out of politics, for to opt out of politics is to opt out of life.

Having said this, we must stress that the small community is not a party cell and it would be utterly wrong to use or manipulate it as such. It is a faith experience. In the course of this faith experience, however, the members are motivated to make what seems in conscience to them the appropriate political option. In the historical profile of the groups above, we gave examples of how they can effectively impact on the political situation.

Communism is a failed system. But so too is Capitalism. It stands condemned by the forty million people who die of hunger or hunger-related diseases every year. A figure equal to the combined populations of Belgium, Australia, and Canada. Suppose we have a family of ten and there is a cake to be shared. If the two strongest were to run off with more than three-quarters of the cake, the remaining eight would be quite rightly enraged at the injustice of it. That, however, is an accurate picture of what is happening on this planet. We have 20% of the earth's inhabitants consuming 80% of its substance. It is a recipe for disaster. Capitalism also stands condemned by the growing millions who are not simply marginalized from even its most minimal benefits, but totally excluded. How can any sane person expect to build happiness in such a desert of discontent?

Total collectivism is not the answer; neither is leaving everything to be somehow regulated by the free market. That seems to me to make just about as much sense as throwing all the pieces of a jigsaw puzzle into the air and expecting them all to fall, so that a perfect picture is formed. The answer lies somewhere in the middle as it always does. If governments renege on their responsibility to govern for the benefit of all, then the law of the jungle prevails.

Good government (the type that a Christian could with a clear conscience support) would in the first place be deeply concerned with the weaker members of society: the old, the sick, the mentally and physically handicapped, the homeless, the unemployed, and so forth. Having given priority to the weak, good government would then preoccupy itself with the well-being of the whole national family. Yet, while being concerned for all, it would not spoon-feed or be paternalistic to anyone; rather would it foster self-reliance and self-respect in every person. Good government would promote a society where there is harmony rooted in justice and obscene inequalities are eliminated. Finally, it would not be so narrowly nationalistic as to be unconcerned about the well-being of other countries on the planet, especially those in the South.

Development

This issue of development is very close to the previous one and has importance for the small communities. I shall begin by quoting a traditional African story from Tanzania:

> The rainy season that year had been the strongest ever and the river had broken its banks. There was water everywhere and the animals were running up to the hills. The floods came so fast that many drowned. Many, except the monkeys who, using their proverbial agility to climb to the treetops, were looking down on the surface of the water where the fish were swimming and gracefully jumping out of the water as if they were the only ones to enjoy the devastating flood. One of the monkeys saw them and shouted to his companion:

'Look down, my friend, look at these poor creatures. They are going to drown. Do you see how they struggle in the water?'

'Yes,' said the other monkey.

'What a pity! Probably they missed out on escaping to the hills because they seem to have no legs ... But how can we save them?'

'I think we must do something. Let us go close to the edge of the flood where the water is not deep enough to cover us and we can help them to get out.'

So the monkeys did that. They started catching the fish not without difficulty, one by one, bringing them out of the water and putting them safely on dry land. After a short time there was a pile of fish lying on the grass, motionless. One of the monkeys said:

'Do you see? They were tired, they are just sleeping and resting. Had it not been for us, my friend, all these poor people without legs would have drowned.'

'They were trying to escape us because they could not understand our good intention but, when they wake up, they will be very grateful because we have brought them salvation.'[3]

Too often in our development work, like those well-meaning monkeys, we completely misread the situation and save the fish from drowning. In other words we help in ways that do more harm than good. In Africa I have seen heavy machinery rotting in ditches for want of fuel or a spare part. I have seen a once proud hospital with trees growing out through the windows of what was formerly the operating theatre. These were projects that expatriates thought would be beneficial for the area, yet failed to involve the local people. They were never the projects of the local inhabitants. They never *owned* them. In the end of the day people cannot *be* developed; they must develop themselves. The question is whether there isn't something outsiders can do to assist this process. If so, well and good.

Workers in poorer nations are not lacking in ingenuity. They can't afford to be; they have to survive. While walking through a township in Nairobi a few years ago, I saw cooking stoves which were manufactured locally and perfectly adapted to the needs of the residents. And in Zimbabwe I was shown a whole array of unsophisticated farm implements and machinery that was most suitable for the environment. Indeed one look at the arts and crafts of Africans would swiftly dispel any reservations one might harbour about their manual skills.

The relevant point about small Christian communities and any such groups, whether religious or secular, is that they are *powerful instruments for development,* because here we have people organized at the grassroots, which seems to me to be the first and most important condition for development. In Sierra Leone at this tragic moment in its history a network of small Christian communities is providing the basis that is making a whole series of development projects possible in the capital, Freetown. Its population has swollen with refugees from the war, and in the midst of all this the groups are engaged in a welter of activities: food distribution, provision of water, literacy work, technical courses, street cleaning, health and hygiene. And their Muslim brothers and sisters have joined in heartily. In Zimbabwe a man engaged in giving courses on self-reliance found that two thirds of the work was done where the communities existed, while in the same country a government development worker was loud in his praise of the groups as facilitators of progress.

Similarly in a variety of places on the African continent the communities are proving impressive support for those stricken with AIDS by getting them to the hospital, summoning the mobile clinic, sharing food, and helping with family chores. Above all they respect the dignity of the victims and encourage them to carry on living and doing something productive if they can. Going among the victims of this dread disease you would expect to find utter desperation. Not so. In a room of terminally ill patients I found music, flowers, visiting friends and family, smiles and peace; all transformed by the power of love. I realized that no matter how tragic things may be, where there is love, there is heaven. There was a playground full of children, every one of whom had received the dire inheritance of AIDS. The person in charge said, 'We are doing our best to keep the children alive in the hope that in the future a cure may be found.' In that situation the laughter of the children was transformed into a hymn to life.

Oh yes, the small Christian communities can be powerful instruments for development. They empower people to speak their word and raise themselves up by their own endeavours. Because of this, groups such as these can provide a sure basis for democracy.

Maintaining momentum in small Christian community

A missionary friend of mine in Zambia once sent a badge to his sister in the United States. On the badge there was a cartoon of a hippopotamus standing upright and underneath there was the caption: *Things desperate: send chocolates.* He had a sweet tooth and said the chocolate kept him going. At least it had the virtue of being a benign stimulant.

We all need something to keep us going. Small Christian communities also require motivation. I have often put the question to groups at home and abroad as to what helped them to maintain momentum. Here are a list of the factors cited:

- the knowledge that of ourselves we cannot persevere and, if we do so, it is ultimately the work of God,
- persisting with conviction through thick and thin,
- knowing that we are called to be a loving open community like the Trinity,
- a strong spiritual life,
- a hunger for the word of God and the Eucharist,
- alert, sympathetic, and challenging leadership,
- full participation in decisions through dialogue and consensus,
- deep reflection on the life of the community,
- ongoing formation,
- concern for others especially for the powerless ones of the world,
- a sense of process,
- regular encounters, 'formal' and social,
- meetings that are varied, interesting, and down to earth, and
- most importantly, encounters that in time gain depth.

Summary

(1) Small Christian communities must be open to diversity and allow for flexibility.

(2) Ecumenism, that we may all be one within the Christian family, is urgent. From this base we then reach out to all religions and to all our fellow human beings.

(3) Our unity will never be uniformity but rather harmony in diversity.

(4) Inculturation, or making the gospel flesh and blood in a particular cultural context, is an important issue for small communities. The groups are the places where it happens, and they are
instruments for bringing it about.

(5) Youth are an integral part of the communities; sometimes cultural reasons may oblige them to have their own groups,
which nevertheless remain open to, and on occasions share
with, adult gatherings.

(6) Even where young people have no trouble in being part of the
ordinary small communities, they may need their own groups
so as to share about their specific problems and take account
of their unique youth culture.

(7) Action is required to solve the Eucharistic famine by adopting
the community model of Church, and by opening up ministry
to a greater variety of people and not just restrict it to male
celibates.

(8) Politics is the dynamic, or active, way in which our whole society is organized. The Church and, consequently, the small
Christian communities must therefore deal with political matters, though they are faith experiences and not political party
cells.

(9) Good government is a matter of looking after the weaker elements of society, fostering self-reliance and self-respect, and
promoting a society where there is harmony rooted in justice.

(10) People cannot be developed but must develop themselves; the
question for outside parties is whether they can do anything to
help bring this about. Again the groups are places where this
can take place and are instruments for bringing it about.

(11) Momentum in small communities is maintained in a variety of
ways. These means are briefly stated above.

Question

Have you to contend with any of the issues mentioned in this chapter in your small Christian community, and how do you cope?
Suggested Bible passage: Matthew 24: 11-13; or Hebrews 12: 1-4.

PART III

What theological vision underlies small Christian communities?

CHAPTER 6

The Church as Communion

In chapter 2 on organization we began by saying that there were three essential elements to the life of the small Christian communities:

- bonding,
- contemplation, and
- reality.

From chapters 2-5 inclusive we have been exploring the rather vast theme of reality, striving to answer the question: *What are small Christian communities, and what do they do?* We now turn our attention to the more visionary aspects of:

- bonding, and
- contemplation.

In doing so, we hope to explore the theological vision underlying the groups. Let us begin with *bonding, or communion.* Where small Christian communities are concerned, this of course has to be the heart of the matter.

In March 1994, I was involved in a workshop in Nairobi. At the beginning the participants were sharing experiences of such communities and I found the story of a young woman called Sylvia of particular interest. 'When I left school,' she informed us, 'I would say that I had the faith. I lived on the outskirts of Nairobi and every Sunday travelled by bus to the centre of the city where I attended Mass at the Holy Family Basilica. But the basilica was very big and I didn't know anyone much. I felt alone. Then going home one Sunday and feeling a bit depressed, I said to myself, I don't have a spiritual friend in the whole world. '

Following this low point of her narrative she went on: 'Soon afterwards I came across a small Christian community in my own area and became a member. With that all changed. In the community I didn't simply hear about love, as in the basilica, I actually *tasted the sweetness of togetherness.* And little by little I grew spiritually, made good friends, and was able to take part in work for my neighbour-hood. I blossomed as a person. No longer am I that girl who trav-elled alone into Nairobi, was lost in the big church, and returned home sad.'

One of the many lessons that this story teaches is the importance of relationships, or bonding. If we are serious about community, there has to be the intention and endeavour to grow in relation-ships. Community consists in this and great happiness can result from intimate sharing.

Community-building, however, can also be painful. As a semi-narian I worked in foreign parts and food was sparse where I was staying. The effect was that I felt hungry all the time. Then one day I was invited out for a meal and went with great relish. There on the table sat this great glorious pot of stew. I gazed longingly at it. Suddenly a tiny head surfaced briefly from its depths. It looked sus-piciously like that of a rat. I nearly lost my appetite.

In community little monsters, our weaknesses, also show their heads and cause problems that lead inevitably to confrontation and conflict which have to be resolved. Otherwise, as we have seen, they can undo the group. Oh by the way, the tiny head proved to be that of a guinea-pig, an animal regarded as a delicacy in many parts of the world. Bearing in mind the difficulties caused by community, why bother with it at all? Would it not be better to maintain a civil distance from one another?

Community like the Trinity

We might take as our starting point the reality of the small Christian community to seek answers to these questions. In the group we find various members who strive through their loving and sharing to become *one.* The roots of this experience, I suggest, we find in the *Blessed Trinity.* Here we have the Father, the Son, and the Holy Spirit who through their intimate loving and sharing are *one God, or one Community.* As they say in Africa, 'There are three dancers but only one dance.'

Now we were created in God's image. In Genesis 1:26-27 we read how God created human beings ' in our own image, after our own likeness ... male and female ...' The statement that we were

created male and female is significant. We were not meant to exist
in isolation. Right from the beginning God's will was that we be *a
community of brothers and sisters without divisions*; there can be differences that enrich, yes, divisions no. The message of scripture is
clear: no barriers. This theme is taken up by Paul, who makes a creative theological leap in Galatians 3:28 to declare:

> There is neither Jew nor Greek,
> there is neither slave nor free,
> there is neither male nor female,
> for all are one in Christ Jesus.

So why must we be community? Quite simply because God is community, and we are created in God's image.

Because of our weakness and perversity, we sinned and brought
division. We marred the unity created by God. This is where Jesus
entered the story and by the will of the Father, the power of the
Holy Spirit, and the free consent of the Virgin Mary came *to restore
harmony*. He is the one who reconciles us to ourselves, to God, to
our brothers and sisters, and to creation round about us. If then the
Christian community has its roots in the Trinity, it finds its *very
being and centre in Christ* (cf. 1 Corinthians 12:27).

The Jesus who cleansed the ten lepers, gave sight to the blind
Bartimaeus and forgave the woman taken in adultery made the
Trinitarian God present in the world (cf. Matthew 1:23; John 14:8-
14). In this latter text of John, for example, Philip says to Christ,
'Lord, show us the Father; that is all we need.' And the answer?
'Whoever has seen me has seen the Father.' He might also have
added 'and the Spirit,' because Jesus is a human way of being
divine and makes the loving God present in the world.

In the sacraments something that we can see makes present
something that we cannot see. In baptism, for instance, the water
which the minister pours and can clearly be observed, makes us
aware of what is invisible, namely, the life of God flowing into the
being of the one receiving the sacrament. So the historic Jesus,
whom people could see, made the loving Trinity, whom they could
not see, present. Christ was a sacrament of the Trinity. *The one who
restored community*; restored God's image and likeness among us.

Christ is risen and no longer with us in the body as he was with
his own people in those far off days. And yet he is still present
among us through his Church. Speaking to its members, Paul said,

'Now you are the body of Christ and individually members of it' (1 Corinthians 12:27). The Church, therefore, is a sacrament of Christ. We can no longer see him in the flesh, but we can see him in the community. So the Church makes Christ present in the world. Indeed as a community of brothers and sisters, who through their loving and sharing become one, it makes the Trinity present. And it is the Church that must now carry on Christ's work of community-building, striving to reconcile us to ourselves, God, neighbour, and environment.

Much too big

The Church, however, is a worldwide reality which is becoming increasingly hard to identify as a community of Christ's followers or as Christ's presence on earth. It is all too big. The picture can begin to blur physically even at the parish stage. One of the places where the true nature of the Church and its identity with Jesus become obvious is in the small Christian community. If to be Church is to experience – and reflect – the intimate life of loving and sharing that characterizes the Trinity, then *this is best achieved in small groups*. It is hard in a parish of thousands or for that matter even in a gathering of a hundred. Hence the importance of small Christian community.

This understanding of small community as a clear witness to the presence of Christ and the Trinity has considerable consequences for making Jesus known and passing on the faith. Indeed I believe that without this witness we are *severely handicapped* in our efforts to do either.

The following story may illustrate the point. I recall a bishop in Africa telling me that his diocese had an excellent catechetical programme for schools. Much of the effort expended, however, was like putting water into a bucket with a hole in it, because the family and the community were in disarray. The reason for this was that the menfolk, searching for work, migrated to the mining areas of nearby South Africa. Owing to the policy of apartheid, which still prevailed at the time, they could not bring their wives and children with them. Some never returned; others had families at home and in South Africa. Either way there was considerable social dislocation. Now what is the good of telling a child at school that *God is love,* if he doesn't experience love in family or small community? It remains a hollow word. The experiential, audio-visual aid of God is missing – the small community.

The need to live Christ in a group is a refrain I have heard in many parts, not least in our own small community in Dublin.

These examples pose searching questions for all Christians:

- Can we even begin to think seriously of announcing Christ (evangelization) or explaining the faith (catechesis) without the witness of the small Christian community to Jesus and the Trinity?
- Isn't the small community an instrument without which we cannot function?

Even the Lord himself went about spreading the good news as part of a travelling community. The love and sharing that he preached, he practised. In short, we need the small communities to do the job of passing on the faith.

Sharing is obviously a key word for community. *The bonding which we are considering* involves sharing all aspects of our lives in common: faith, commitment, worship, ideas, vision, good works, and material possessions. It is a complete sharing of mind, heart, and hand. In more formal terms we might speak of a sharing that is spiritual, intellectual, intuitive, emotional, and practical. Oftentimes when we talk of sharing, we are thinking of food, money, or some such item. As we see, it is much more than that.

It can of course be a matter of life's necessities. During a workshop in an African country that was undergoing a severe drought, we were reflecting on Acts 4:32-37, the passage that speaks of the early Christians as being 'one in mind and heart.' Starvation was staring those people in the face, yet a poor farmer spoke up saying: 'This passage challenges me to go back home and share even the little that I have with others.' Here was love that cut to the bone.

It is worth noting at this point that bonding is not just something which is pastorally necessary, but that equally, according to experts in the field, is it *a deep psychological need* for every human being. There is this hunger in all of us to belong.

Commitment

From the realities that we share, as expressed above, we might perhaps single out commitment for special comment, because *it is the*

*heart and soul of community generally, and particularly of the small
Christian community.* By this, community will either stand or fall.
That it presupposes *faith* in Jesus the Saviour goes without saying.
There can be no question of Christian commitment without belief in
him, because it calls for *a persevering and total dedication to gospel values.* There has to be commitment on the part of each member of the
community and of the community as a whole.

This also presupposes *conversion* – that the members have taken
seriously the responsibilities that come with baptism. At some
point in their lives they have made a U-turn away from evil and
towards God. But then the consequences of that conversion have to
be lived, so that every day they struggle to become a little less self-
ish, a little more generous. Faith isn't simply a matter of ideas in the
head, it translates into love in action. In other words there is the
continuous effort, as Paul puts it, to grow to the full stature of
Christ (cf. Ephesians 4:13). There we find the life programme and
real challenge for every Christian: to become so Christlike that one
day he might be able to say with Paul '… it is no longer I who live,
but it is Christ who lives in me' (Galatians 2:20).

When sharing on conversion and commitment with groups, I
find it important to remind myself and those to whom I am speaking that this does not mean that small community is composed of
angels. It is made up of sinners who in their brokenness often fall
(cf. Proverbs 24:16), yet they steadfastly refuse to stay down. They
always rise again to seek reconciliation with God and neighbour.
Community is constantly being built up through continual reconciliation. St John Bosco used to tell his boys that the tragedy lay not in
falling, but in failing to rise again. And Dom Helder Camara writes:
'At the great judgment seat the Lord may say to someone: 'How
horrible! You fell a million times!' But all is salvaged if that person
can say: 'Yes, Lord, it really is frightful! But your grace helped me to
get back on my feet a million and one times.'[1]

This leads to my own understanding of commitment as, *Never
ceasing to try.* And when I think about it, community members like
Miguel often come to mind. From Monday to Saturday he spent
long hours working in his South American factory for a paltry
wage. He also spent long hours travelling to and fro on overcrowded
buses. Yet on Sunday he laboured up the steep slopes of the Andes
to share the good news of Jesus Christ with children. 'When Sunday

comes,' he once told me, 'I often feel ill and not at all like going up the mountain. But how good the Lord is because, when I overcome my weariness and go, I always feel better.' Of such dedicated people surely is the kingdom of God.

We have seen, therefore, that all community, or *bonding*, whether merely human or Christian has its roots in the Trinity. Furthermore Christian community is the body of Christ. He is its centre. He gives it its being. And these realities find their most obvious expression in reduced groupings such as the small Christian communities. Indeed they make real the vision of Vatican II as stated in the *Dogmatic Constitution of the Church* (*Lumen Gentium*), no. 4 (cf. also 10, 11, 12), which calls on the Church to be:

> '... a people brought into unity from the unity of the Father, the Son and the Holy Spirit.'

The whole vision underlying the small communities springs from the depths of the Blessed Trinity. Through Christ it impacts the Church and, as we shall see presently, breaks its boundaries to flow out and transform all of creation.

Summary

(1)   Having dealt with the reality of small Christian community in chapters 2-5, we now turn to the remaining themes of bonding and contemplation, so as to answer the question: What theological vision underlies the small Christian community? We begin with bonding.

(2)   Where small Christian communities are concerned, bonding or communion has to be the heart of the matter.

(3)   Community building can be beautiful, because of the fellowship, yet painful because human perversity and weakness intrude.

(4)   So why community?

(5)   Because the Trinity is community and we humans are created in God's image and likeness.

(6)   God created us as community. We sinned and brought division.

(7)   Christ came to reconcile us to ourselves, God, brothers and sisters, and environment. He healed division, made God present in the world, was a sacrament of the Trinity.

(8)   The Church, a sacrament of Christ, continues his work of reconciliation and community building.

(9)   This work is best realized through reduced groupings such as the small Christian communities. They can be easily seen. They allow people to live a life of intimate loving and sharing like the Trinity, and can actively pass on the faith.

(10) The small communities link so as to become a communion of communities. The members then experience both the intimate group and the wider network – a complete experience of Church.

(11) In the groups there is a sharing of all aspects of life: faith, commitment, worship, ideas, vision, creativity, friendship, good works, and material possessions.

(12) Commitment is the heart and soul of community.

(13) The small Christian communities make real the vision of Vatican II, which calls on the Church to be: 'a people brought into unity from the unity of the Father, the Son, and the Holy Spirit' (*Lumen Gentium, Dogmatic Constitution of the Church*, no. 4).

(14) The theological vision underlying the small communities springs from the depths of the Trinity and through Christ impacts the Church and the whole world.

Questions

(1)   Have you any experience of being in a small group, religious or other, and what in the light of the foregoing chapter are your thoughts about it?
      Suggested Bible passage: Acts 4: 32-37.

(2)   How does the Trinitarian model of Church as communion relate to your own experience? Or does it relate at all?
      Suggested Bible passage: John 17: 20-26.

(3)   Commitment is never ceasing to try. Do you agree?
      Suggested Bible passage: Mark 10: 17-31.

CHAPTER 7

The Kingdom of God

The *bonding* which has its origins in the Trinity and explains the small Christian communities extends beyond the confines of the Church to the whole of creation. This takes us into the realm of the kingdom of God. The Church is part of this kingdom, as we shall see, but not the whole of it. It extends to all of creation and into eternity. To complete our picture we must follow the vision.

The most important thing for Jesus in his ministry was the kingdom of God and its justice (cf. Matthew 6:33). The word *Church* is only used twice in the gospels (Matthew 16:18; 18:17-18) while Christ speaks frequently of *the kingdom*. Pope Paul VI describes the kingdom as 'the absolute good' to which everything else must defer (cf. *Evangelii Nuntiandi, The Evangelization of Peoples*, no. 8). If, therefore, the kingdom is the priority for Jesus and if it is the absolute good, it is crucial that we consider the question: what exactly is the kingdom of God? A further query then would be: how does it relate to the Church generally and, more specifically, to the small Christian communities?

I realize that there is a problem with the word *kingdom*. For some it would carry masculine connotations. However, the terms used to replace it so far seem to miss out somewhat on theological content, so we must wait upon experts to help us in this respect. Meanwhile I have opted to stay with the traditional expression.

There is a two-line poem by Hugh O'Donnell that has a teacher address a class so:

> Attention!
> Today, I will finish creation.[1]

That person was setting out to define the mystery. Where the kingdom of God is concerned, Jesus never defines it, precisely because it is a mystery. Nevertheless he says many things that shed light on this great reality. But first of all let us turn to the Old Testament.

The kingdom in the Old Testament

The vision of the kingdom is deeply embedded in the scriptures commencing with the Old Testament.[2] Abraham sought out a new land and Moses 'a land rich and broad where milk and honey flows' (Exodus 3:8); so the earliest understanding of the kingdom was the rather basic one that it was *linked to territory*.

The prophets Isaiah and Jeremiah took this a step forward by declaring that in the promised land there would be *a privileged place for the poor*. Justice was not simply a matter of fasting while trampling on the little ones of the earth. Indeed such penance was worthless (cf. Isaiah 58:1-12).

In 587 BCE the Jews were taken captive to Babylon. This for them was a catastrophe because *their* land *was* the kingdom of God, and God dwelt in the Temple. Now they were cut off from both. Hence their lament:

How can we sing the Lord's song
in a foreign land? (Psalm 137)

God wasn't there to listen. During those awful times, when their vision had been shattered by exile, Isaiah encouraged his people to hope again (cf. 42:1), and they began to get the idea that the vision of the kingdom was not tied to territory, but was *interior*, an empire of the heart:

Thus says the Lord:
'Heaven is my throne
and earth is my footstool;
what is the house which you would
build for me,
and what is the place of my rest?
(Isaiah 66: 1-2).

In the centuries after the exile a powerful mood that the end was near swept through the Middle East. And the notion that the kingdom of God would not be fully realized in this world grew; it would stretch on into the *hereafter*. It was in this period too that the actual expression 'kingdom of God' was used for the first time (cf. Wisdom 10:10).

We see, therefore, how the understanding of the kingdom gradually developed in the Old Testament.

The kingdom in the New Testament

Jesus began his mission in Galilee with the clarion call: 'The time is fulfilled, and the kingdom of God is at hand; repent and believe the gospel' (Mark 1:15). The kingdom is the main theme of his mission, the 'good news' he brings. Christ does not define what he meant by it because, after all, it is a mystery (cf. Matthew 13:11; Mark 4:11; Luke 8:10); however we are told many things about it in the New Testament. Here we give a selection of the salient points. The kingdom:

- is the priority (cf. Matthew 6:33; Luke 12:31).
- lasts forever (cf. Luke 1:33; 2 Peter 1:11).
- is present in the world, yet is still to come (cf. 1 Corinthians 15: 12-28).
- means preaching the word (cf. Matthew 13:1-23; Mark 4:1-20; Luke 8:4-15).
- is near, 'within you' (cf. Luke 17:21).
- contains the good and the bad (cf, Matthew 13:24-30).
- grows from small beginnings (cf. Matthew 13:31-32; Luke 13:18-19).
- is a leaven (cf. Luke 13:20-21; Matthew 13:33).
- imposes obligations to love and forgive (cf. Matthew 18:23-35).
- welcomes all comers (cf. Matthew 20:1-16).
- is doing the will of God (cf. Matthew 6:10).
- means being always ready (cf. Matthew 25:1-13).
- calls on us to be bold and decisive (cf. Matthew 11:12; Luke 16:16).
- is 'where the blind see, the lame walk' (Luke 7:22) and where 'I was hungry and you fed me, thirsty and you gave me a drink' (Matthew 25:35).

Sometimes in the New Testament the kingdom seems to be identified with Jesus himself: Jesus *is* the kingdom (cf. Matthew 16:28; 19:29; 21:9; Mark 9:1; 10:29; 11: 9-10; Luke 9:27; 18:29; 19:38; Acts 8:12; 28:31; Revelation 12:10).

John does not speak very much of the kingdom. But again he would seem to identify it with the person of Christ in all those *I am* statements that he makes in his gospel. 'You want to know what the kingdom is like?' John would seem to say, 'Then look at Christ.' The following would be examples of this:

- I am the bread of life (John 6:35).
- I am the gate for the sheep (John 10:7).
- I am the Good Shepherd (John 10:11).
- I am the light of the world (John 8:12).
- I am the real vine (John 15:1).
- I am the way, the truth and the life (John 14:6).
- I am thirsty (John 19:28).
- I am who I am (John 13:19) – despite which he washes the disciples feet.
- I am who I am, you cannot go where I am going (John 8:24).
- I am not from this world (John 8:23).

We have just said above that the kingdom welcomes all comers. And that is true. Yet from the Beatitudes we gather that there is a special place there for the poor, those who mourn, the meek, those who hunger and thirst for justice, the merciful, the pure in heart, the peacemakers, and those persecuted for righteousness (cf. Matthew 5:1-11). 'These,' to quote a friend of mine who put it rather graphically, 'are the "A" team in the kingdom of God.' If an earthly manager were to select such an outfit, she would undoubtedly be summarily fired!

Paul, of course, envisions the kingdom as *a new creation*,' where neither circumcision nor uncircumcision counts for anything (Galatians 6:15); and this is the same as John's understanding of it as *a new heaven and a new earth*' (cf. Revelation 21:1) – a complete transformation of the old realities.

Looked at negatively, the kingdom is not simply about:
- money, as in the case of the rich young man (Mark 10:17-31),
- places of honour, which we learn from the rebuff of Jesus to the mother of James and John (Mark 10:35-45),
- earthly authority, gathered from Jesus' reply to the question, 'By whose authority do you speak?' (Mark 11:28),
- worldly considerations such as taxes (Mark 12:13-17),
- buildings and structures: even the Temple is to be destroyed (Mark 13:1-2).

The spiritual dimension is supreme, though the earthly is given its due weight.

The foregoing provides a scriptural profile of the kingdom of God, and, as we see, there is no attempt by Christ or anyone else to define this multi-faceted reality. It is a matter of faith. Yet it is clearly something of infinite value worth sacrificing all to attain here and hereafter.

We might attempt to *summarize the vision* in this manner: the kingdom is:

* 'a new heaven and a new earth.'
* the priority.
* God's rule prevailing in the world.[3]
* the person of Jesus: his mind, heart, and values.
* wherever there is harmony rooted in justice.
* all that is good, gracious and, therefore, God-revealing.
* openness and tolerance.
* present and yet to come.

Harmony would be the sustained note of God's kingdom, though in it we find some strange bedfellows indeed, as the beautiful images of Isaiah strikingly illustrate:

> The wolf shall live with the lamb,
> the leopard shall lie down with
> the kid,
> the calf and the lion and the
> fatling together,
> and a little child shall lead them.
> Isaiah 11:6.

Two defining moments

There have been two great defining moments in the history of the Church. The first was when that great pastoral genius, Paul, made the breakthrough of realizing that Christianity was not simply for the Jews but for all peoples, and took the good news to the gentiles. He also realized that, though the Christian religion grew out of Judaism, it was something totally new (cf. 2 Corinthians 5:17; Ephesians 4:4; Colossians: 3:10-11). The second great moment has occurred in our own times, when Vatican II and John XXIII flung the windows of the Church wide open and pointed to the kingdom out there that needed continuous building up.

The Church is part of the kingdom; it is not the whole of it. As we said above, *wherever we find goodness* or wherever there is *harmony rooted in justice*, the kingdom is there. It doesn't matter whether those involved are Christians, Muslims, Jews, Hindus, or Buddhists;

we as a priority will support them. After all, if there is a bridge to be built, there is no such thing as a Catholic, Muslim, or Hindu bridge. Bridges are ecumenical and permit all sorts of people to cross a river in safety.

In December 1992, I had an experience that brought home to me this universal nature of the kingdom; indeed I have referred briefly to it in a meeting recorded in chapter 3. I enjoyed the privilege of visiting some Buddhist communities in Thailand. One of them, the Tamkaenjan group, was situated on the banks of the River Kwai, just below the famous bridge. What I noticed particularly about the members of this community was their deep reverence for God's creation. 'Look here,' said Paiboon, an animator of the group, 'some undergrowth was cleared away from this area so that we could replant it, and immediately this profusion of grass sprang up to prevent erosion. The more I see of creation the more I become aware of the greatness of the Creator.'

As you would expect, the community farmed in an environmentally friendly fashion, and had eight of their members going throughout Thailand on bicycles, sensitizing people on the subject of the rainforest. These made their listeners acutely aware of what a terrible loss the destruction of this facility would be. It could mean the disappearance forever of natural and medicinal resources that human beings desperately need. Cures maybe for cancer, AIDS, and ebola. Who could tell? Many secrets of the rainforest still remained to be unearthed. In addition to these activities there was a school for very poor boys, some of them Cambodian refugees with sad tales to tell, to whom the group was communicating the noblest of ideals.

There was a flock of geese that belonged to the group cavorting on the river. In fact two ganders fought a pitched battle in the vivid moonlight over some likely goose while I was there, and had to be quarantined in the interests of nocturnal tranquillity. However, the community didn't eat the geese or the fish that abounded in the River Kwai, because they were strictly vegetarian. The flock was there purely so that they could rejoice in God's creation.

Most enlightening of all, however, were my conversations with Paiboon. Straight from the start we found we had a lot in common. Neither of us was locked into his own position and we were eager to learn. I told him that the most important thing for Christ was the kingdom of God. I tried to shed some light on what that entailed for Christians, explaining how it meant upholding goodness and working to build a better world where there was harmony rooted in justice. In short we were talking about the creation of *a civilization of love*.

He had no problem in relating to all of this. Actually the core Buddhist teaching is:

• not to do evil,
• to cultivate goodness,
• and to purify one's mind.

'How can you know God,' he asked me on one occasion, 'since God cannot be known?'

'Well, God cannot be known,' I fumbled, somewhat surprised by the question, 'in the sense that no matter how much we know there is no end to what we still have to learn. But it doesn't mean that we cannot know anything at all about God. Creation speaks of God, as you yourself have shown so clearly, and our Bible tells us that God, who has given us this wonderful world, is a God of love. In fact it says God *is* love. So we can know God through other people, for when we experience love from our fellow human beings, we are experiencing God. Now if we experience something, that is truly knowing. The best road towards knowing God is through living community, as you are doing.'

There was a long silence. 'What do you think of what I've just said, Paiboon?' I asked.

'It's all very new to me,' he replied.

Quite out of the blue the next day he volunteered the following: 'I've been thinking of what you said. Now I believe that God is compassionate. That's just another name for love, so what you said makes sense.'

At that moment I had an image of Christ looking at him and saying with wonder, 'You are not far from the kingdom of God' (Mark 12:34).

I was not able to stay with the group as long a I would have wished. What I saw, however, led me to believe that, although the Tamkaenjan Community was not Christian (and I don't intend this to be patronizing), it certainly could from our point of view be described as a kingdom group. Their priority was Christ's priority.

Here was goodness, openness, and harmony rooted in justice. It patently showed the kingdom flourishing beyond the confines of Christianity, and brought home to me the need to be *ecumenical* in the broadest sense by linking up with all people of goodwill to build a better world.

A personal vision of kingdom

Besides the commonly held perceptions of the kingdom, we all have our personal vision, or vocation. It may consist simply in someone doing an ordinary job of work and struggling to bring up a family as good Christians and honest citizens. There is much that passes for ordinary that is quite extraordinary. I feel that legions of great saints have led hidden lives, sanctifying themselves by doing a whole array of minute chores thoroughly and with love over a lifetime. Few get the chance to live high-profile lives. A doctor I know has quietly given her whole life, sacrificing the possibility of marriage and family, to the service of the African people. Our private aspirations we of course integrate with the wider panorama of the kingdom of God.

Our doctor no doubt suffered, and that too is an integral part of our destiny (John 12:24). To gain the kingdom we shall have to die and rise again with Christ. While hanging on the cross, Jesus felt desolate and abandoned, though in reality the Father never abandoned him. Through Jesus God entered history and endured the pain of the cross, because Jesus is a human way of being divine. The astonishing truth, then, is that the Almighty shared in our human lot of suffering – so much for the myth of a God that is distant and uncaring. In the desolation of Christ the Father risked failure, but Jesus did not fail. Even as he cried out, 'My God, my God, why hast thou forsaken me?' (Matthew 27:46) and passed painfully through the gap of death, he clung with his fingernails to hope. He trusted in his *Abba* (a most endearing term for 'father') and in the promise of the kingdom – the kingdom that he had so convincingly preached, and bore witness to, in the course of his ministry. And God vindicated his trust and the whole purpose of his life by raising him from the dead. The cross is what we did to Jesus; the resurrection what the Father did. Along this path, sooner or later, all of us must follow Christ. And we too will have to hang on with our fingernails, hoping and trusting, as we give our final answer to the great question of love.

As well as having our own personal vision of the kingdom of God, we can also have our own particular examples and images of it too. Those that come to my mind relate to the women of the world, to begin with those of my own family. After those there were the laundry women in South American *barrios* who sweated over the clothes of the rich so that their families might survive. And the mothers of Soweto, who during the bus boycotts in the struggle against apartheid, arose in the dark and walked for long hours to their domestic tasks in the luxurious homes of white South Africans in Johannesburg, and, then, at the end of the long trek home in the evening, there was supper to cook. These were the unsung heroes of the freedom struggle. Also, there were the women of famine-stricken Mozambique, already mentioned, who trudged across the border with Zimbabwe, bearing enormous loads of grass which they sold to buy bread for their starving children. Great sacrifices intertwined with the thousands of seemingly lesser sacrifices of cooking, cleaning, and caring that help to keep this world on course. Up to this, women have largely borne the burden of life. It is now time for all to fully join the struggle. Justice must be done.

Justice

Justice is to the kingdom what oxygen is to life. They have to go together. Jesus does not merely say, 'Seek first the kingdom,' but adds significantly, 'and its *justice* ...' (Matthew 6:33); we cannot have the bonding without the righteousness.

Justice, according to the Bible and the documents of the Church, means having right relationships with:
- self,
- God,
- neighbour, and
- environment.

It is total in its approach to unity. And isn't the expression *right relationships* merely another way of saying community or kingdom? These realities are closely interwoven.

Oftentimes, when we speak of justice, we are thinking only of economic justice: fair returns for our work, proper conditions in industrial plants, and so on. Justice, however, is much more than that because it touches all aspects of our existence.

I once heard a woman of African origin say at a meeting in a São Paulo *favela*, or poor district: 'I am oppressed three times over. I'm oppressed because I am poor; I'm oppressed because I am a woman; and I'm oppressed because I am black.' I was somewhat surprised to hear her say, for example, that she was oppressed because she was a woman. The men in the district, after all, were passionately involved in issues of justice. And yet this woman, and others as it turned out, felt oppressed because of their gender. So apparently the menfolk still lacked a clear understanding of the full nature of justice.

If relations with persons and, consequently, with God are marred by discrimination, justice suffers.

Respect for the environment is also an integral part of justice. There is the divine community of the Trinity, the human community, and the community of creation – all intimately bound together.

The little poem called *Stupidity Street* by Ralph Hodgson,[4] already referred to in chapter 3, shows how the things of nature are so precariously linked together. The poem is all the more remarkable because it was written early in the twentieth century, when the public was certainly not as environmentally conscious as it is today. For the convenience of the reader I quote it here once more.

> I saw with open eyes
> Singing birds sweet
> Sold in the shops,
> For people to eat,
> Sold in the shops of
> Stupidity Street.
>
> I saw in a vision
> The worm in the wheat,
> And in the shops nothing
> For people to eat;
> Nothing for sale
> In Stupidity Street.

In her fine book, *The Cry of the People*, Penny Lernoux makes the same point, showing the havoc that reigns when multinational corporations are allowed to rape the rainforests. She writes as follows:

> But perhaps the worst example of the multinationals' slash-and-burn methods in the Amazon is provided by the Italian

conglomerate Liquigas, which purchased 1.4 million acres in the heart of Xavante Indians' territory. Sixty Indians died when the military forced them to move from their land, and now only a few charred stumps remain of the forests where the Xavantes once hunted, the land having been seeded in grass. Like most Amazon cattle ranches, the Liquigas project produces only for the export market, using an airstrip big enough to accommodate chartered 707s that fly direct to Italy with the meat packaged in supermarket cuts and the price stamped in lire.[5]

A final point about our description of justice, given above, is necessary. It might seem presumptuous to put right relationships with self before right relationships with God. But the reasoning behind it is that, unless we can relate properly to ourselves in the first place, we are severely hindered in relating to God, neighbour, or environment. *Community begins in my own heart. And so too does the kingdom.*

Now, what we *do*, as opposed to what we *say*, about justice is of tremendous importance when we come to announce the gospel. The Synod of Bishops meeting in Rome, 1971, had this to say:

> *Action* on behalf of justice and a participation in the transformation of the world appear to us as *a constitutive dimension* of preaching the Gospel, or, in other words, of the Church's mission for the redemption of the human race and its liberation from every oppressive situation (italics mine).[6]

So in the matter of passing on the faith, as in ecumenism, the query is never, shall we, or shall we not, do something about justice? The only question to be asked is *what exactly* are we going to do? What is the best course of action in our circumstances? During the days of apartheid in South Africa, for example, when an individual missionary stood up in a pulpit and condemned the system, expelling that person from the country was an easy matter. But when an episcopal conference spoke out as a body, how could the authorities possibly counter that? This was to prove a most effective strategy. We already gave examples of telling action by small Christian communities in Kenya and Zambia in the face of thorny political situations.

Action for justice is not solely a matter of shaping national events. Quite the contrary. In fact it is unlikely that people will eventually immerse themselves in these more difficult, and sometimes dangerous, issues, if they are not doing the work of justice in more humble ways. The places to begin are in the home and neighbourhood. If relationships in these areas are not right, with what credibility can we operate further afield?

Option with the poor

In the 'kingdom of justice and peace,' which the preface speaks about in the Eucharist on the feast of Christ the King, an option with the poor is a given. The Church itself made an option with the poor at Puebla, Mexico, 1979. In doing so it was simply following Christ whose own choice it clearly was:

> The Spirit of the Lord is upon me,
> because he has anointed me to preach
> good news to the poor.
> He has sent me to proclaim release to captives
> and recovery of sight to the blind,
> to set at liberty those who are
> oppressed,
> to proclaim the acceptable year of the Lord
> (Luke 4: 18-19).

It has been common to speak of an option *for* he poor, yet many economically deprived folk prefer the expression option *with* the poor. It seems to them less condescending. Besides *with* the poor is where everyone belongs in any case, and it is the *haves* who benefit from solidarity with the *have-nots* rather than the reverse. The poor proclaim the good news to the rich, recall them to a true sense of values, and disabuse them of the spurious notion that diamonds are forever.

Jesus was one with the poor, stood solidly with them in their just cause, loved them, shared with them, and lived simply himself. Well, was he not born in a stable? Did he not die stripped of all on the cross? And during his arduous ministry, unlike the birds of the air and the foxes of the field, was he not often without a place to lay his head at night? His simple lifestyle is a challenge to every Christian. The evils of the world exist precisely because people fail to love, share, and live simply. The Irish development agency,

Trócaire, had a large poster some years ago that boldly proclaimed: LIVE SIMPLY SO THAT OTHERS CAN SIMPLY LIVE. It says it all. On this planet of ours, the greed of the minority deprives the many of life; the misguided few mistakenly think that they can create an oasis of happiness in a desert of deprivation and discontent. Above all, if we want to have an authentic vision of the world, we must view it through the eyes of the poor as Christ did.

I find from experience that *the option with the poor* and what it means is a stumbling-block for many, and in discussion it can die the death of a thousand rationalizations. Who are the poor anyway? It is a question often asked, never, ironically, by the poor themselves. I once heard a student remark that, instead of talking endlessly about this issue, one would do far better to go live and work with the deprived and learn from experience, which was what he did himself. I'm sure he was right. However, it is not surprising if we find this option with the poor bitter medicine. So too did the apostles. Mark tells us:

> And they were exceedingly astonished,
> and said to him,
> 'Then who can be saved?'
> Jesus looked at them and said,
> 'With mortals it is impossible,
> but not with God;
> for all things are possible with God.'
> (Mark 10: 26-27)

Jesus, I think, is not saying that we can hang on happily to our millions and expect salvation; rather is he telling us that by the grace of God we can make an option with the poor however difficult it may seem.

Obviously, though, when we come to consider who the poor are, *the materially poor* first spring to mind; the vast majority of the world's population who don't know where their next meal is coming from. Then in the Old Testament the Hebrew terms for poverty ('ani' and 'dal' in particular) convey a notion of powerlessness. So the poor are *the powerless ones*. The state of powerlessness, of course, usually goes with material want. And, finally, they belong to the little ones of the earth, or 'anawim', *who opt with the poor* and adopt a simple lifestyle. Incidentally, when we talk about poverty, or simplicity of living, we are not referring to misery. We would want every human being to have sufficient means to procure a home, food, and clothing; to be able to educate her children and provide for legitimate recreation. There is no virtue in degradation and filth. Jesus proclaimed that he came so that we might all have life and have it abundantly (cf. John 10:10).

In the light of the foregoing, I am often baffled by references to what is called the middle-class Church. I realize, of course, that this may be a convenient sociological rather than a theological description. But looked at theologically, there is no such Church. There is only the Church of the poor (the materially poor and those who identify with them), a community of the faithful, all equal through baptism. So we should not lightly use the expression *middle-class Church.* Surely classism is as abhorrent to the Christian as racism or sexism, and the feminist movement has made us all aware of the importance of being sensitive in the language we use.

In the foregoing, we have shared some thoughts as to what is meant by our Christian priority, the kingdom of God and its justice. At the outset we also posed the further question regarding how the kingdom related to the Church generally and, more specifically, to the small Christian communities. We shall now consider this query.

The kingdom and the small Christian communities

The Church is called upon to be salt and light in the world, or an agent for the fostering of goodness (cf. Matthew 5:13-14). Because of this, it ought to be *a powerful expression* of the kingdom on earth and *an effective instrument* for promoting it , but it is not of course the whole of the Lord's domain. This stretches to the farthest reaches of creation and beyond into everlasting life. The kingdom of God was there before the Church, and it will still be there when the Church is no more.

A point we made in the previous chapter again becomes relevant. In terms of witness where can we put our finger on the Church? Where can it be clearly seen? In a parish of thousands? Even in a group of 100? No. The Church is most obviously discernible in small Christian communities; in practice it is these that are at the cutting edge of witness and action. *The small Christian communities are the most effective agents for building the kingdom of God and its justice.* They witness palpably to it. They forge it. We have cited numerous examples that bear this out.

The examples also show the relevance of the groups to the justice issue. They are down-to-earth and not floating about in an other-worldly haze. If justice is about right relationships, they give witness to, and are fine instruments for, fostering it in society.

Another name for small Christian community is *basic* Christian community.

This means that the group is:

- of the poor.
- involved in actions from the grassroots.
- a place that invites fuller participation by all, for example, women, youth, and children.
- immersed in real life issues.

In short the community is context and instrument for justice.

Elsewhere we referred to the small community as context and instrument for evangelization, catechesis, and inculturation. If we were to explore the possibility, we would also find that it is context and instrument for communication and morality. Are these not all about relating to people effectively and properly?

* * *

And so we conclude our theme on *bonding.* In the course of our reflections we have seen how this phenomenon of bonding, which we find in the small Christian communities, has its roots in relationships within the community of the Trinity (cf chapter 6). From there the harmonising impact bursts out upon, not only the members of the Church, but all humans – humans created in the image and likeness of God, three in one (Genesis 1:26-27). Indeed the whole of creation, or the kingdom of God, can mirror this unity of the Trinity (cf current chapter).

Christ, whose body the Church is, was the great restorer of community at the heart of these developments. And all of this found its clearest expression in the small communities which combined to form a communion of communities.

It is important for groups to know the context and theological underpinning for their experience. I shall yield the last word in this regard to Peter, a coordinator of a small Christian community in Sunyani, Ghana. At the conclusion of a workshop, he commented:

We were like ants in our small Christian communities. We saw our own little patch of ground but not the wider landscape. Now we have a vision. We see where we fit into the Church and the kingdom and can go forward feeling more confident. I feel very happy.

Summary

(1) The bonding which has its origins in the Trinity and explains the small Christian communities extends beyond the Church to the whole kingdom of God.

(2) To complete our theme we must follow the vision.

(3) The kingdom of God (and its justice) is the priority for Christ and his followers.

(4) What is the kingdom ? And how does it relate to the Church and the small Christian communities?

(5) The kingdom is scriptural (ample references provided from the Old and New Testaments).

(6) To summarize, the kingdom is:
- the priority.
- God's rule prevailing in the world.
- the person of Jesus, his mind, heart, and values.
- wherever there is harmony rooted in justice.
- all that is good, gracious and, therefore, God-revealing.
- openness and tolerance.
- present and yet to come.

(7) We can have our own particular vision of the kingdom, which ties in with our calling, and our own special images of it too.

(8) The kingdom and justice are inseparable.

(9) Justice is right relationships with self, God, neighbour, and environment.

(10) Action for justice is an essential element of preaching the gospel.

(11) The Church is not the whole of the kingdom of God, but part of it. It should give *powerful witness* to that kingdom and its justice and be an *effective instrument* for promoting them.

(12) Because the Church is so extensive, these roles of witness and instrument are more *concretely and efficiently* realized in small Christian communities.

(13) Thus ends our *bonding* theme.

Questions

(1) What do you understand by the expression *kingdom of God*? How does your understanding fit in with your experience? Suggested Bible passage: Matthew 6:25-34.

(2) What does the kingdom mean for you personally? Any relevant images or examples?
Suggested Bible passage: Matthew 13:1-23; or Matthew 13:24-43; or Matthew: 13:44-51.

(3) From your experience what is your understanding of justice?
Suggested Bible passage: Isaiah 58:1-12; or Matthew 25:31-40.

(4) What can small Christian communities and groups do about justice in your area?
Suggested Bible passage: Luke 1:46-55.

(5) How do you feel about the option with the poor?
Suggested Bible passage: Luke 4:16-21; or Mark 10:17-31.

CHAPTER 8

Contemplation

At the outset we pointed to three essentials for the life of small Christian communities, namely, bonding, contemplation, and reality. Having completed reality and bonding, we now turn to contemplation. Contemplation is the spiritual backing that buttresses all that we do in small Christian communities, and so we include it among the more visionary aspects. It is the contemplative atmosphere in which they operate that prevents the communities from becoming merely social action groups.

In the autumn of 1994, I gave a workshop in a Dublin parish which was hoping to launch small communities. I have already referred to the occasion in another context. In the course of the session it became obvious that the parish was a most apostolic one. There was an activity group to meet virtually every human need: the elderly, sick, handicapped, youth, deprived ... And yet the participants felt something vital was missing. They identified it as being a contemplative dimension; their action needed a more intense spiritual backing.

Similarly, in 1992, a priest who was a chaplain to Young Christian Workers and Students in Canberra, Australia, said, 'We have been missing out somewhat on contemplation.'

Contemplation would embrace:
- the Eucharist,
- prayer,
- word of God,
- reconciliation, and
- reflection.

The Eucharist

Many Christian denominations would regard their communities as being *Eucharistic*. This has huge implications for them, because the

Eucharist is above all a *celebration of unity*, of the efforts they are making in their families and small groups to be one. When the presiding minister raises the host, they are powerfully challenged to be body of Christ as the bread is body of Christ. 'Though we are many, we all become one, for we share in the one bread and the one cup' (1 Corinthians 10:16-17). How can they possibly partake of these mysteries and fail to be united? If people riven by class division celebrate the sacrament, it becomes an empty gesture. With the Christians in Corinth who are falling into this error, Paul is blunt: 'It is not the Lord's supper you are celebrating' (1 Corinthians 11:20).

The Eucharist then is a clarion call to Christians to be body of Christ, and to the whole world to be a community of brothers and sisters in the image of the Trinity. Like the mystery of the Trinity the Eucharist demands a world where there is universal collaboration and equality among people. It is, therefore, intimately linked not just to purely spiritual issues, but also to political, social and economic ones. The justice element here is obvious. Christ generously breaks bread with the whole world, and we are challenged to do the same, especially with the 40 million who die of hunger or hunger-related diseases every year. As pointed out earlier the number corresponds to *the combined populations of Belgium, Canada, and Australia.* And this catastrophe is befalling people *in a world of plenty.* As often happens, also, most of the victims are children. Indeed countless little ones are denied the right to be born at all. Never will they be able to rejoice with the psalmist in saying, 'I thank you Lord for the wonder of my being' (Psalm 139:13-14). When we talk of breaking bread, we are not simply referring to real bread; we are speaking too of breaking the bread of unity and fairness with all.

While I was working on this book, my brother passed away, and I had the consolation of giving him Holy Communion for the last time. When I arrived at his bedside on the afternoon before he died, he whispered to me insistently, 'Communion, Jim, ... Holy Communion.' Although I thought the hospital chaplain must have already given it to him, I decided to administer the sacrament. However, I later learned that because his mouth and throat were so sore from chemotherapy, it was felt he could not swallow the host. He had not received; hence his agitation. I gave him a tiny portion of the bread with some water. He smarted at the touch of the water, but managed to receive in the presence of his family. I shall never forget the peace that then descended upon him. I began to see a little more clearly what Jesus meant when he declared: 'I am the bread of life' (John 6:35).

If we conclude from the foregoing that the proper place to celebrate the Eucharist is in community, no one will be surprised. And yet I feel that too often, particularly in the affluent world, the assembly is composed of an amalgam of individuals – well-meaning individuals, but individuals nonetheless. This was brought home to me clearly by an incident that happened in Ireland. I was giving a retreat to some university students and was removing the vestments after celebrating the Eucharist, when a young man approached and spoke to me. 'I haven't been to Mass for a long time,' he informed me, 'and I've had a difficulty with the Eucharist. I'm only here because my friends pretty well dragged me here. But the Mass we had today was different from anything I've experienced before in my life. It really moved me.' I have to say I was somewhat surprised by his words. Quite honestly, the celebration was nothing out of the ordinary. As I pondered what he had said later, however, I concluded that the whole experience was transformed for him by the fact that he was celebrating with his intimate friends. It was truly a celebration of community, in community.

Finally I should like to add that not only is the Eucharist something that challenges us to live in harmony; it also helps us to do so. It is food for the weak as we journey through this hazardous world. During his life there was nothing Christ liked to do more than sit down and have a meal with his friends and tell stories, or parables. It was one way that this person-for-others gave himself to his neighbour. On the night before he died that was exactly what he did, sat down and had a meal with his disciples while his enemies plotted his downfall out there in the darkness. This, however, became a very special meal in which he gave us his flesh to eat and his blood to drink, so that we might have life, and asked us to go on as long as time lasts doing this in his memory (cf. 1 Corinthians 11:23-26). The next day he was going to shed that blood to the last drop for us on the cross. And that is why the *meal* and the *sacrifice* are always linked together in the Christian memory. The Eucharist and the cross are one, the place where true lovers meet, and a powerful source of grace which irrevocably binds people together in life and death.

The word of God

Regarding the word of God, it is important to realize that it doesn't
take precedence over the life experience of the members of a community. They must look first at their own lives and try to make
sense of them in the light of the scripture, or Christ-event, just as the
early Christians did. The Spirit of Christ is not only found in scripture but also in the Christian community of every era. As Carlos
Mesters, a Dutch scholar and missionary working in Brazil, puts it:
'The word of God is not just the Bible. The word of God is within
reality and it can be discovered there with the help of the Bible.'[1] So
ideally to use the scriptures effectively, a community should meet
around the word, yet relate the realities of their own lives to the
text: 'Their struggle becomes part of the picture.'[2]

Yet another point on the use of scripture. According to some
experts, the best way to deal with the Bible is to ask how the passage under consideration helps or challenges *me*. What issues does
it raise for *me*? I may then share my insights with the other members of a group *without preaching at them*; in a Bible-sharing we
avoid preaching. We express our thoughts in a spirit of 'this is how
this passage challenges *me*' or 'this is what it says to me ... maybe it
helps you, maybe not ...' And we don't argue. We respect what the
members say and do not set them right. There is a difference between
a Bible discussion, when we strive to thrash things out together,
and a quiet, meditative Bible-sharing.

In 1991, I was conducting sessions in Sierra Leone, on small
Christian community as usual. The following is an entry in my jour-
nal for March 15th:

> Today we had an intensive day-long workshop in the village
> of Benduma, towards the east of the country. It took place in
> a chapel made of slats and covered with a grass roof. It was
> quite an experience. The whole Christian community was
> present, including the children. The village chief, a Muslim,
> complete with flowing garment and fez, also attended. In
> addition to the children within, all the remaining youngsters
> of the village were jostling outside in an effort to peer
> through the slats to see what was going on.
>
> Every so often an adult would whoosh them all away, yet
> they'd be right back like bees to a honey pot. And there was

the buzz too. The catechist was reading ponderously from the Bible. Beneath the lectern a boy was carrying on, just a little. In reality the children were as good as gold. Anyway, the catechist snapped the Bible shut and gently, but firmly, cracked the lad on the head with the word of God. After this momentary episode the reading proceeded with all due decorum. It's amazing what happens when one is struck by the word of God!

I tell this story to make what seems to me an important point. We must not use the word of God to beat other people over the head with and take bits out of context to prove our arguments. Scripture was not intended for this purpose. It is there to question, strengthen, and affirm us while we travel as pilgrims along the arduous, yet exciting, road of life.

An interesting phenomenon of our times is that the Bible is to be found back in the hands of the laity. It is no longer the preserve of just the cleric or the scholar. This is a wholesome development because it was written for ordinary people by ordinary people in the first place. So they can often be more at home than intellectuals with the stories, myths, symbols, songs, poems, drama, and powerful word pictures that are the very stuff of which the scriptures are made. They can indeed be utterly fascinated by it all. In this context I recall the story of a venerable African lady who loved reading. Above all she devoted herself to the scriptures. As she sat with her Bible one day, a neighbour asked why she didn't give more time to other literature. To which she replied: 'Other books I read, but this book reads me.' I have seen a learned article of about twenty pages that made the same point. Not as memorably.

Sometimes there is a person in small Christian community who has a good knowledge of the Bible. How can he best help the group? One thing is certain: he must beware of taking over the meeting and turning it into a Bible lesson, thereby stifling the spontaneity and participation of the members. He could help, however, by briefly providing something of the historical and cultural background of the passage being shared.

We see Ernesto Cardenal do this very skilfully with the peasants of Solentiname in Nicaragua. The community is about to discuss Matthew 6:7-15, which deals with the Lord's Prayer. Taking the words:

And in prayer
do not heap up empty phrases.

Ernesto goes on to explain, 'The translation is rather, "Don't go blah-blah-blah-blah". The Greek word that Matthew uses is *battalogein*, which is like saying blah-blah-blah-blah.' Then dealing with the expression:

Our Father who art in heaven,

he further elaborates: 'Jesus didn't really use the word "Father". Jesus said in Aramaic *Abba*, which is "papa" and that was probably always the word he used in speaking of God.'[3] With this instruction the stage is set for a most absorbing reflection by the participants.

Regarding the power of the word of God, I had a striking experience in Zimbabwe. We had been reflecting in a community on John 17, and afterwards a little sister approached me. 'Father,' she began, 'I was really impressed by those words of Jesus, "I pray not only for them, but also for those who believe in me because of their message." Here was Jesus going out to die, and I realised that he was thinking of me at that moment. The poor soul, he prayed for me. I felt like crying. And, father,' she went on, 'I work as a chaplain in the mission hospital. Many people there are dying of AIDS ... young people ... some of them relatives ... and they are in mortal fear of death. Now I'm going to be able to say to them, Don't be afraid. Look here in the gospel; Jesus prayed for you! There's no need to be afraid.'

Prayer

The most common form of prayer practised in the small Christian community is *spontaneous*, that is, *comes straight from the heart*. Usually this prayer follows on from a life-related reflection on the word of God and is broken by long pauses for silent meditation. Spontaneity in this case certainly does not mean a thoughtless blurting out of sentiments; the term simply means that no set or formal prayers are used.

Following a reflection on Matthew 25:31-40 ('I was hungry and you gave me food, I was thirsty and you gave me drink), for example, someone might pray like this:

Almighty God, help us to realize the dignity of every human being, without exception. Jesus considers as done to himself

whatever we do even to the least of our brothers and sisters
Help us, Lord, to treat all your people with respect. May we
assist them when they are in need. Lord, hear us.

At a recent meeting of our Dublin community, basing his intervention on the words of Jesus, 'Strive to enter by the narrow door;
for many, I tell you, will seek to enter and will not be able' (Luke
13:24), Andrew prayed thus:

Lord, the scripture asks us to enter heaven by the narrow
door, asks us to be counter cultural, to go against the tide, not
to seek the way of easy popularity. Help us, Lord, to be nar-
row-door people insofar as we are just , not sold on material
goods, and use the things of earth well. Help us also to lead
others through the narrow door, the way of simplicity of
lifestyle, of gentleness, of compassion, love, and of selfless-
ness. Lord, hear us.

Many of the spontaneous prayers quite rightly centre on the
concerns of people's lives: the recovery of a sick relative, work for
the unemployed, success in an examination, freedom from hunger,
disease, and oppression. And always these prayers are accompanied by the realization that the members have to do something
about them.

The more simple the context, the more skilful folk can be at com-
posing their own prayers. In economically deprived countries, the
people are often quite at home with spontaneous prayer. By con-
trast, affluent nations, as we noted elsewhere, are conditioned by
instant tea, instant coffee, and microwave ovens. The instant society
can fail to understand that a facility for spontaneous prayer cannot
be acquired overnight.

An example will help us to realize that there is a process
involved. It is taken from a group in Ireland. When they first started, this group, which was rather youthful, discussed problems a
great deal. They tended to shy away from anything religious. Since
they had been formed as a small Christian community, however,
the coordinators would read some passage of scripture related to
the problem under consideration. The reading at that stage was not
an integral part of the meeting, but something of an afterthought
that could at a pinch be discarded. And that was how matters stood
at the beginning.

After some sessions the animators began to invite all to join hands and recite The Lord's Prayer to finish off the meeting.

Almost imperceptibly, some spontaneous prayer crept in. Usually it was the animators who did it. But gradually others began to imitate them and acquire the skill. The word of God also became a more integral part of the proceedings.

Private prayer

Small Christian community members, in addition to their prayer life in common, usually feel a deep need for private prayer. There is no one way of doing this. The important thing is to focus on God, and the method we use seems to be secondary. Whether it be silent or oral is a matter of choice. Commenting on Matthew's phrase, 'In your prayers do not babble as the pagans do' (6:7), Charles de Faucauld says:

> In this counsel you [the Lord] are telling us that for mental prayer words are not necessary: it is enough to kneel there lovingly at Your feet, contemplating your majesty with every admiration, every desire for your glory, consolation and love, in short with every movement of our hearts that love prompts us to. Prayer, as St Theresa tells us, consists in not speaking a lot, but *in loving a lot*.[4]

So prayer is above all a matter of *relationship*. It means being an intimate friend of God. Charles De Foucauld's understanding of it might be described as *thinking of God with affection*.

This description is not too unlike 'the methodless prayer' of Jane de Chantal and Francis de Sales. Jane is quoted as saying the following:

> The great method of prayer is to have no method at all. When the Holy Spirit has taken possession of the person who prays, it does as it pleases without any more need for rules and methods. The soul must be in God's hands like clay in the hands of a potter so that God might fashion all sorts of parts. Or the soul must be like soft wax to receive the seal's impression, or like a blank tablet upon which the Holy Spirit can write the divine will.

And she goes on to say:

> If going to prayer, one can become pure capacity for receiv-

ing the Spirit of God, that will suffice for any method. Prayer must happen by grace and not by artfulness. Go to prayer in faith, remain there in hope and go out only by charity which requires simply that one act and suffer.[5]

Prayer is *a simple waiting before God*. Sometimes in our busy lives we are so weary that the efforts to marshal our thoughts proves even too much. Not to worry. We can remain affectionately in the presence of God. Quite rightly does Jane remark that prayer is a grace anyway, and we cannot give it to ourselves. All we can achieve is to dispose ourselves to do it and leave the rest to the Lord. It is helpful also to recall the words of Paul who reminds us that, when we fail, the Spirit within us can act on our behalf:

Likewise the Spirit helps us in our weakness; for we do not know how to pray as we ought, but that very Spirit intercedes with sighs too deep for words. And God, who searches the heart, knows what is in the mind of the Spirit, because the Spirit intercedes for the saints according to the will of God. (Romans 8: 26-27)

There are those who find it helpful to pray by reciting a mantra such as *Maranatha* (Come Lord Jesus) over and over again, as a means of focusing the attention on God. They usually do this sitting in an upright position, breathing easily and with eyes closed. However, psychologists tell us that the human attention span is 20 minutes maximum, so we mustn't be surprised if distractions keep on intruding. Personally I feel that the phrase *a continual fight with distractions* would sum up the story of my own prayer life.

Reconciliation, or the ability to forgive and be forgiven, is vital to the life of small Christian communities; if we cannot be reconciled, they will obviously fall apart. As we learn from the gospel, there must be no limit to the number of times we are willing to forgive (Luke 17:4). We are all a mixture of saint and sinner and, because it is so, we offend one another, sometimes without even meaning to. Conflict, as we already pointed out, is inevitable in community, and, if not dealt with , can destroy a group. Furthermore reconciliation is not just a matter of forgiving others; accepting pardon ourselves can be an equally thorny issue.

Reflection we also singled out as of importance to community life. By this we are of course referring to meditative prayer, but it goes further than that. In a small Christian group the members must reflect on all aspects of their lives in common. We recall these aspects: worship, faith-sharing, commitment, vision, exchange of ideas, friendship, good works, and participation in material resources. Many small, or even religious communities, have come to a standstill because they got themselves on to a treadmill of activity, yet ceased to reflect on what they were doing.

In conclusion, then, we must reaffirm the great importance of the whole area of contemplation where small Christian communities are concerned. Contemplation without outreach is spurious, but outreach without contemplation is also flawed.

Summary

(1) Having dealt with the themes of reality and bonding, we turn finally to contemplation.

(2) Contemplation is essential to the life of small Christian communities.

(3) In contemplation we include: Eucharist, prayer, the word of God, prayer, reconciliation, and reflection.

(4) The Eucharist, meal and sacrifice, celebrates and creates community.

(5) The Eucharist is a clarion call to unity.

(6) It is a call to break the bread of justice with the whole world.

(7) The most effective way to use the Bible is to ask how it questions, or what it says to, me.

(8) There must be no preaching at, or putting down of others with, the scripture.

(9) A resource person can help a small community in its Bible-sharing by briefly filling in for them something of the historical and cultural background of a scripture passage.

(10) The most common form of prayer in a small community is shared and spontaneous (straight from the heart).

(11) Some people may have to grow into such prayer gradually, particularly in the affluent world.

(12) Private prayer is also important for group members.

(13) Any method that puts one in contact with God is valid, whether or not words are used.

(14) Methodless prayer, or a simple waiting on God, is another possibility.
(15) The Spirit too pleads on our behalf and it is good to remember this.
(16) Reconciliation, or the ability to forgive and be forgiven, is important for the lives of small Christian communities.
(17) Reflection on all aspects of the groups' life in common is also crucial.

Questions

(1) Does your group give due importance to contemplation?
Suggested Bible passage: Luke 6:12-16; or Luke 18:1-8.
(2) What does the Eucharist mean to your community?
Suggested Bible passage: John 6:41-58; or 1 Corinthians 10:16-17; or 1 Corinthians 11:17-22.
(3) Does your group relate the word of God to life and life to the word of God?
Suggested Bible passage: John 1:1-14; or 1 James 1:22-25.
(4) How does your small community pray?
Suggested Bible passage: Matthew 6:5-15.
(5) From your experience would you say that reconciliation is important for your community?
Suggested Bible passage: Luke 7:36-50; or Luke 17:1-4.
(6) Does your group reflect frequently on all aspects of your life in common (faith, commitment, worship, ideas, vision, creativity, friendship, good works, and material possessions).
Suggested passage: Acts 15: 1-41, the disciples evaluate.

CHAPTER 9

Spirituality

Closely related to the subject of contemplation is that of spirituality. *Spirituality is a lived experience of faith.* We could say too that it springs from whatever motivates us in our relationship with self, God, neighbour, and environment: a hunger for peace and justice or a concern for God's creation would be good examples. I feel attracted to the above description because it is so in touch with life. Besides, looking back over one's faith experience and selecting the salient points provides a sure basis for reflection. Some of the features have already emerged in the course of this book, and we don't have to belabour these again, but merely draw attention to them.

Trinitarian

In a small Christian community we find various members who through their loving and sharing become one. The roots of their experience we find in the Trinity where the Father, Son, and Holy Spirit share intimately and are one God, or one community. We are created in the image and likeness of God (cf. Genesis 1:26-27) and are, therefore, most like God when we live community. All this we considered in chapter 6. So first and foremost the spirituality, or lived experience, of the small Christian community is Trinitarian. It finds its reason for existing and explanation in the Blessed Trinity, and the consequences of this flow out beyond the confines of the Church to all creation in the endeavours of people to build the kingdom of God and its justice, to live simply, and make an option with the poor. So the communities are *ecumenical* in the widest possible sense.

A vital relationship with Christ

The group is also in a palpable way the body of Christ (cf. 1 Corinthians 12:27). It is centred in Christ the Saviour. The word *save*

in the Synoptic Gospels has the meaning of a healing done by Jesus;
he is the healer of divisions, the creator of community. The members have a vital relationship with Christ, *or strive to live Christ* (cf.
Galatians 2:20-21), and this is another outstanding feature of their
spirituality. Jesus is a real friend. They are always conscious of his
presence. The mind, the heart, and the values of the Saviour are the
light of their lives; a fact that is most opportune. There is a great
need, and John Paul II has stressed this, to make Christ known as
we approach the third millennium. The Pope speaks of 'a new evangelization.' We seem to be caught up in many questions and issues
in the Church which, though important, are not the heart of the
good news. The core of the gospel is:

    For God so loved the world
    that he gave his only Son,
    so that whoever believes in him shall not perish
    But have eternal life (John 3:16).

I have seen this joyful text in the most unusual places. Sometimes
a person holds it aloft at great sporting events for the benefit of the
crowd and TV cameras. Usually they are positioned behind a goal
and raise their placard following a score. Then there is a mighty
cheer. It would be nice if it were for Jesus who lived, died, and rose
to save us. But people generally have other quite mundane things
on their mind at that moment. However, maybe the text does regis-
ter fleetingly with the people present, as it always does with me.

We mentioned the proliferation of sects in Latin America earlier.
One of the reasons for this is that in faith sharing they focus directly
on Christ. And despite their other-worldly, alienating nature, they
impart a sense of fellowship and self-worth to people whom society
marginalizes or even totally excludes.

The presence, action, and guidance of the Holy Spirit.

I find that modern small communities are as conscious of the presence, guidance, and action of the Holy Spirit as their forebears were
in the New Testament (cf. Acts 15:28). Occasionally the interventions of the Spirit in the groups can seem dramatic, as some earlier
examples indicated, but generally it is a case of gentle accompaniment which can be either affirming or challenging as the situation
demands.

Integration of faith and life

Since Vatican II with its theme of the Church being 'present in' and not 'apart from' the world (cf. *The Pastoral Constitution of the Church in the Modern World*), the necessity to integrate faith and life has been highlighted. In the past this was not always the case. There is a verse in Ireland that brings out this fact graphically. It goes:

> Paddy Murphy went to Mass,
> Never missed a Sunday.
> But Paddy Murphy went to hell
> for what he did on Monday.

It seems the poor man failed to make the vital connection between belief and practice with not so pleasant consequences. Faith in Jesus who died and rose to save us is not just a matter of ideas in the head. These must translate into love in action. The integration of faith and action is a noteworthy feature of the groups.

The word of God, prayer, the Eucharist, reflection, reconciliation

We have seen how concerned the communities are too about constancy in reflection on the word of God, prayer, celebration of the Eucharist, reflection, and reconciliation. This expresses itself in creative liturgies like the example we gave from Perth, Australia, in chapter 3. It is a great mistake to hawk stereotyped liturgical celebrations around the world, as if Mass in Toronto, for instance, were no different from that in Dombo Tombo or Waga Waga. Just to take a small yet significant point: in many countries the faithful stand while reciting the 'I confess' at the beginning of Mass, whereas in much of Africa this would be unthinkable. Pardon you ask for on your knees.

A new person

A new person is emerging among the members of the groupings. People are not seen any more in terms of gender, race, age, social condition, or colour, but rather as human persons, children of God, sisters and brothers in Christ. These are the realities that give individuals their inalienable dignity and they are to be found in a crippled child, begging on the street of some teeming city, just as surely as in the President within her palace. In this the members are beginning to realize the vision of St Paul:

> There is neither Jew nor Greek,
> there is neither slave nor free,
> there is neither male nor female,
> for you are all one in Christ Jesus. (Galatians 3: 28)

Fostering cultural awareness

Not only do the small Christian communities promote the common dignity of every person; they attend as well to what may be distinctive by fostering cultural awareness. This does not simply mean hearkening back to the past. Cultures are dynamic. They encompass the present and future as well as the past. However, this does not mean that the myths, stories, dramas, proverbs, poems, songs, dances – in a word 'folklore' – of a people are allowed to slip into oblivion. Not at all.

In a Kenyan group the members were asked to share what their experience of small Christian community was. One man began by telling a story. 'Long, long ago,' he told us, 'a tribe of people lived in this land called the Jumas. They had very large heads indeed. So when they fell over, they could not get up. A little like a beetle that gets turned on its back and then thrashes the air with its legs and gets nowhere. If another Juma did not come and lift the prostrate one up, he would die. They were always eager to give one another a hand. But sometimes it happened that no one came by and the one who had fallen died. Eventually the whole race decided to live underground, where there would be more support, and another people called the Kikuyus, that's us, came to live on the land left vacant.' My mother told me this story. I learned about community at my mother's knee before ever hearing of Christian community. Even as a little fellow I knew the importance of lending a hand, so that we might all survive. What small Christian community has taught me is that I must be ready to give a helping hand not just to my friend, but also to my enemy. This is a big lesson.

I found this a most effective use of folklore to make a Christian point. A case of the culture nurturing Christianity and Christianity the culture. The tale was from the past, yet was adapted imaginatively to the present, and constituted a challenge for the future.

Spirit of perseverance

A characteristic of the groups that has most impressed me is their spirit of perseverance through thick and thin. It always brings to mind the words of the gospel: '… the one who endures to the end will be saved' (Matthew 24:13). When we encounter a group that is truly community, it tends to be either long-term or permanent; our Dublin one has now been going for fourteen years. It started with a little band of school-leavers and various of them are now married and have children. We have had our ups and downs, yet we are still here. The explanation? We have already cited factors that make for perseverance in groups, but the members of our community have no doubt that, above all, it is the work of the Spirit. Of course, another important reason why people keep on coming back is that they find in the group the strength and motivation to go out and struggle to lead a Christian life. Without the spiritual backing it would be much more difficult.

And yet, despite being long-term, small communities must never allow themselves to become cosy or complacent, and they must be prepared to die should they discern that this is what the Lord wants. Needless to say, death for the Christian group is never a question of extinction. They die only to give birth to something new; to live in other communities. As John's gospel says so beautifully:

> Truly, truly, I say to you,
> unless a grain of wheat falls into the ground and dies,
> it remains alone;
> but if it dies, it bears much fruit. (John 12:24)

When some of the believers were scattered by persecution from Jerusalem following the death of Stephen, the Church spread to Antioch and elsewhere. Indeed it was at Antioch that the followers of Jesus were first called 'Christians' (cf. Acts 11:19-30).

Low profile

The groups tend to be low-profile. This is so both in terms of what they are and what they do. Their style is not flamboyant; they are the leaven silently transforming the general population. Oftentimes, more especially in their beginnings before some form of linking has taken place, they can be quite hidden. In Bathurst,

Australia, I met two communities that were situated within a few streets of each other and still unaware of each other's existence, and at the moment here in Ireland there are hundreds of disconnected faith-sharing groups. Part of the explanation for the reticence, and we referred to the phenomenon before, is that they enjoy a new-found autonomy, or breathing space, and fight shy of being seized upon and organized by some over-zealous individual or movement. Networking and structure are desirable. But these developments have to be organic and come from the grassroots, and, of course, never take precedence over people or deprive small Christian communities of their relative autonomy, or freedom.

Likewise small Christian communities are by and large ordinary in the things they do. It's a question of striving to be a Christian at home, in the factory, or in the school. It's about visiting the sick, burying the dead, helping in the fields, working with youth or the elderly or the handicapped. Oh there can be heroic things too. I have had the privilege of having had friends who gave their lives for Christ and their brothers and sisters. Mostly, however, it is a matter of doing little things well and with love over a long time. It is 'the little way ' that made an extraordinary saint of Thérèse of the Child Jesus.

A hunger for knowledge of the things of God

The spirituality of the groups is characterized by a hunger for knowledge of the things of God. The dynamic of the communities seems to lead inevitably to this. The members become aware that there is much to learn. In our Dublin community, for example, various of the members, male and female, have taken night courses in theology. This they did at the beginning of their working lives at considerable cost to themselves in time and money. Such was their thirst to know more about Christ and his message. And the thirst continues.

Laughter and the love of friends

Last, but by no means least, joy and laughter and fun are integral parts of the spirituality of small Christian communities. Even in the normal meetings there is a lot of *craic* (the Gaelic for 'fun', pronounced 'crack', though it has nothing to do with the prohibited substance of the same name!). Then there is much social toing and froing: engagements, weddings, newly-born babies, holidays, outings, parties, picnics, pilgrimages, casual getting together for coffee and a chat. One of the great joys for our Dublin group, as I have indicated, has been the arrival of babies Jamie, Ciara, Niamh, Conor, Luke, Ian, Ben, Clara, Katie, and Joss. The future of the community is assured!

As well as being brothers and sisters in Christ, humanly we are friends, so there is great support for the individual member from the whole community. But there is also a practice in the group that each member has a special spiritual friend (*anamchara*, or soul-friend, in Gaelic) for a designated period. These pairings are picked out of a hat, and they meet from time to time for a meal, or coffee, and a chat. The main purpose for this is to share faith and help one another spiritually. This we find an extremely useful supplement to the support the community as a whole provides. When the designated period is finished, new partnerships are arranged, so that little by little we grow to know one another really well.

How do other spiritualities fit in with that of the small Christian community? What of someone who is already a devotee of the Salesian, Franciscan, Ignatian, Carmelite, or Celtic way to holiness? In no case can I find that their particular emphases cannot be accommodated by the spirituality of the small Christian communities. It is simply that they enhance it at certain points. The insistence of Francis and Jane on loving kindness and the need for a warm family spirit causes no problem for a group. Quite the contrary. Nor does Francis' love of poverty and his option with the poor. Equally Ignatius' finding God in all things and discerning God's will in decision-making are meat and drink to a life-related community. The Carmelite stress on the humanity of Christ and on God being found among the pots and pans presents absolutely no problem. Celtic spirituality, too, with all its intertwining symbols is nothing if not communitarian, or Trinitarian. And there are other salient features of the Celtic way together with a love for the Trinity, all of which fit in with the spirituality of the small Christian communities: the centrality of the word of God, the importance of creation and redemption, and of the nearness (incarnation) of God and eternity (balanced by a sense of their transcendence, or awesome distance); then, of course, there is the fondness for the supernatural, and prayer that is down-to-earth. It seems to me that, not surprisingly, all Christian spiritualities have the same fundamental points in common. Where they differ is in emphasis, style, and methods of prayer, but these too can of course be important. People vary so much in what they find amenable. Horses for courses.

Brainstorming

In our community we carried out a brainstorming on the subject of the spirituality, by reflecting on some of the more pronounced aspects of our experience. I shall conclude by giving some of the statements made, in no particular order, simply as they came. Most of the points would be implicit in the foregoing. They may, perhaps, sound more personalized and may even add their own original wrinkle here and there. My italics will seek to emphasize key elements:

- 'What comes to my mind first, is *the joy* experienced and, indeed, *the fun* we've had down the years.'
- 'I really *felt intimacy* in this community.'
- 'What strikes me about the spirituality of the group is *how simple* it has been; just a matter of sharing our lives. It even seemed mundane at times; I'm sure it never was really.'
- 'The community was the holy ground where I was to find *acceptance and support*.'
- 'You had to be *true to yourself* here.
- 'The group responded to *our deeper nature as social animals*.'
- 'I always felt *the Spirit was near*, mostly in the background, but we had our surprises!'
- 'And *Jesus* too was *always there for us*.'
- 'I found the group a place where I could *share faith*, and that was most important in a world that's growing ever more secular.'
- 'In family *love is natural*; in community it is *a matter of faith*; more difficult and, perhaps, more meritorious.'
- '*The process whereby I love myself was nourished on the way to loving God*.'
- Our community, if we think about it, has come through *an incredible journey* during which we all *grew spiritually and humanly*.
- 'Let me put it this way, "*I feel loved in this group*".'

And so our sharing on the subject of the spirituality of the small Christian communities is completed. The elements highlighted are those that emerge from the lived faith experience of these communities. Here too, of course, ends our theme of *contemplation* which is part of the triad with bonding and reality.

Summary

(1)   Spirituality is closely related to the sphere of contemplation.
(2)   Spirituality is a lived experience of faith.
(3)   The spirituality of small Christian communities involves:
   •   being Trinitarian, or finding the roots of unity in the Trinity.
   •   having a relationship with Christ - to live Jesus.
   •   sensing the presence, action, and guidance of the Holy Spirit.
   •   integrating faith and life.
   •   being constant in sharing the word of God, prayer, the celebra-
       tion of the Eucharist, reflection, and reconciliation.
   •   Creating 'the new person' – valued for fundamental human
       and spiritual qualities.
   •   fostering cultural awareness.
   •   having a spirit of perseverance.
   •   hungering for knowledge of God and the things of God.
   •   being joyful, intimate, accepting, supportive and keen to share
       spiritually.

Five of the above points would, I suppose, embrace all of the others
in some way, namely, that the small Christian communities are:
   •   Trinitarian, or make real the intimacy of the Father, Son, and
       Holy Spirit.
   •   groups that integrate faith and action.
   •   constant in meditating on the word of God, prayer, and the
       celebration of the Eucharist.
   •   living cells that foster cultural awareness.
   •   filled with joy.

Questions

(1)   What does the word 'spirituality' mean for you, and how does
      it apply to your life?
      Suggested Bible verse: Micah 6:8.
(2)   From the experience of your own small Christian community,
      what would you add to, or subtract from, the points made
      above regarding the spirituality of the small Christian com-
      munity?
      Suggested reading: Genesis 1:26-27; or John 17:20-26; or Gal-
      atians 3:26-29; or Galatians 2:20-21; or Vatican II, *Dogmatic
      Constitution on the Church*, no. 4.

Conclusion

And so, having dealt with the themes of bonding, contemplation, and reality, we conclude this work on small Christian communities. We shared the adventure of seeing the harmony that finds its origins among the persons of the Blessed Trinity flow out to human beings and to all of creation, right up to its confines and beyond into the hereafter. All of this is the domain of God, or the kingdom of God. This was the vision that inspired the great apostle of Ireland, St Patrick, who concludes his well-known *Breastplate* thus:

> I bind on to myself the name,
> The strong name of the Trinity;
> By invocation of the same,
> The Three in One and One in Three;
> Of whom all nature hath creation,
> Eternal Father, Spirit, Word;
> Praise the Lord of my salvation –
> Salvation is of Christ the Lord! Amen.

Before finishing, I should like to draw attention to the importance of the small-community formula for all those people of goodwill who want to build a civilization of love. The fundamental points made in this volume have a significance that go far beyond the Christian faith. In short, it is when people cease to be mere individuals or groups and fuse into reduced and recognisable communities that we have a phenomenon which can change the world. A group fused around the Risen Lord in Jerusalem almost 2,000 years ago, and the world has never again been the same.[1] Groups fused in Paris in 1879, rallied by the ideals of Liberty, Equality, and Fraternity. The Bastille fell, and the rest is history.[2]

What would the key elements of the community formula be in a non-Christian setting? I suggest they would be as follows:

167

- *bonding* (the intention of the members gradually to relate at depth),
- *an ethos , or wholesome value system,* (with which the participants would have to keep in touch by constant meditation and reflection),
- and *reality* (the bonding and reflection would need to result in outreach, or action, to build a better world).

Regarding the ethos, the great religions will of course already have one; we already noted, for example, that of the Buddhists:
- not to do evil,
- to cultivate goodness, and
- to purify the mind.

The ethos of a purely secular community might be motivated by the loving desire to cherish the environment, oppose violence, or protect God's creatures, or some such commitment. Then in the cause of good all such communities should strive to network so as to uphold and support one another in their endeavours.

In chapter 2 we pointed out that there is a sociological difference between a group and a community, which did not mean that we devalued the groups. Indeed communities ought to see them as allies in the struggle, and link up with groups of all kinds, whether religious or secular, that are doing something for the betterment of society.

A story that I tell has somehow endeared itself to many people, and I repeat it here:

> In the early 1960s Pearl, a frail little old lady in her 70s, was demonstrating outside the White House against racism. She was arrested and tried.
>
> 'My goodness,' said the judge, 'you are such a frail little lady, I don't know what to do with you, even though you have been breaking the law.'
>
> 'You must do what your conscience tells you,' retorted Pearl feistily, 'just as I do what my conscience tells me.'
>
> Well, the judge did what his conscience told him, and sent her for a stint in prison.
>
> While in prison she had a heart attack and was been driven in an ambulance with flashing blue lights and wailing siren to the nearest hospital. She came to and asked what had hap-

pened. The attendants told her.

'What hospital are you taking me to?' she enquired.

They named the hospital.

'Does it admit Americans of African origin?'

No, it was for whites only.

Despite her condition she stubbornly refused to go, and the ambulance driver, swearing profusely, had to reverse his vehicle and speed to a hospital at a much greater distance that accepted folk of all races. And having survived the prison and the heart attack, back she went – to demonstrate against racism in front of the White House.

Twenty years later, I met Pearl at a meeting protesting the nuclear threat. To me she seemed a most experienced, wise, and holy person, so I thought I would put an important question, perhaps *the* most important question, to her. 'Pearl,' I asked, 'what is happiness?' Without hesitation, out of her long experience and great wisdom, she replied, 'Happiness is *belonging*.' And that, I feel, is as good a note as any on which to end this book.

APPENDIX

Passages for Bible Sharing

Community/Church
- Genesis 1: 26-27. 'Let us make human beings in our own image...male and female God created them.'
- Psalm 133 (132). 'Behold how good...when brothers and sisters dwell in unity!'
- Matthew 5: 13-14. 'You are the salt of the earth...'
- Matthew 7: 15-28. Matthew's idea of Church...false prophets within...a community that *does* the will of God.
- Matthew 8: 18-27. Church - a community that *follows* Jesus come what may.
- Matthew 10: 5-42. Church *missionary* - God sends Jesus - Jesus sends community to the rest of the world - world must respond.
- Matthew 11: 28-30. Church - a community that takes on the yoke of Christ - appears heavy - not so really.
- Matthew 12: 22-28. 'Every kingdom divided against itself is laid waste...'
- Matthew 13: 24-58. Good and bad found in the Church - weeding expeditions dangerous - a sorting out to take place at the appropriate time.
- Matthew 18: 7-35. Seriousness of following Jesus.
- Matthew 19: 16-30. Give up anything in order to *follow* Jesus.
- Matthew 21: 28-32. *Doing* is crucial in the Church community.
- John 15: 5-10. 'I am the vine...'
- John 15: 11-17. '...love one another as I have loved you.'
- John 17: 20-26. 'I pray that they may all be one.'
- Acts 2: 42-47. The early Christian community.
- Acts 4: 32-37. The early Christian community.
- Acts 9: 1-8. 'Saul, Saul, why do you persecute *me*?'
- 1 Corinthians 11: 17-34. Division in community.
- 1 Corinthians 12: 14-27. '...you are the body of Christ.'
- Ephesians 5: 29-31. 'The two shall become one.'
- 1 Thessalonians 4: 13-8. Anxiety over death.

Community/Eucharist.
- Luke 22: 14-23. 'Do this in remembrance of me.'
- John 6: 35-58. 'I am the bread of life...'
- 1 Corinthians 10: 16-17; '...we who are many are one body...'
- 1 Corinthians 11: 17-22; '...it is not the Lord's supper that you eat.'
- 1 Corinthians 11: 23-26. 'Do this in remembrance of me.'

Commitment/Conversion
- Matthew 24: 11-13. 'But the one who endures to the end will be saved.'
- Luke 9: 57-62. 'Leave the dead to bury their own dead...'
- Luke 13: 22-30. Enter by the narrow gate.
- John 12: 20-26; '...unless a grain of wheat falls into the earth and dies...'
- Mark 10: 17-31. The Rich Young Man.
- Luke 19: 1-10. Zaccheus.
- Acts 9:1-13. The conversion of Saul.
- Galatians 2:20-21; '...it is no longer I who live, but Christ who lives in me...'
- Galatians 3: 1-5. 'Having begun with the Spirit, are you now ending with the flesh.'
- Galatians 3: 28-29. 'There is neither Jew nor Greek...'
- Galatians 5: 11. Stand fast.
- Galatians 5: 13-15. 'For you were called to freedom...'
- Ephesians 4: 1-16. Attaining 'to the measure of the stature of the fullness of Christ.'
- Hebrews 12: 1-4; '...let us run with perseverance...'
- 1 Peter 3:13-18. '...make a defence to anyone who calls you to account for the hope that is in you....'

Dialogue/Discernment
- Ecclesiasticus (Sirach) 5: 9-13. Firm in resolution, careful in speaking.
- Ecclesiasticus (Sirach) 23: 7-14. Wisdom in silence.
- Ecclesiasticus (Sirach) 37: 16-18. Communication through silence.
- Matthew 12: 33-37. 'For out of the abundance of the heart the mouth speaks.'
- Luke 1: 26-38. Listening and speaking well.
- Luke 2: 41-52. 'listening to them and asking them questions...and his mother kept all these things in her heart.'
- Luke 24: 13-35. Jesus listens.
- John 4: 1-30. Jesus listens.
- Acts 15: 1-41. The apostles enter into dialogue.
- 1 Corinthians 2: 6-16; 4: 6-7; 6: 1-8; 7: 10-12; 12: 4-11. Discernment with the help of the Spirit.
- 1 Corinthians 16: 13-14. 'Let all that you do be done in love.'
- Ephesians 4: 10-16. '...speaking the truth in love...'
- James 3: 1-12. Listening and speaking well.

Diversity
- Genesis 1. Diversity in creation.
- Matthew 13: 47-50. Fish of every kind gathered in the net.
- 1 Corinthians 12: 4-31. The body of Christ has many parts.
- Mark 9: 38-41. Openness.

Environment/Creation
- Genesis 1 and 2. God found everything that had been created good.
- Psalms 8, 19 (18), 24 (23), 29 (28), 50 (49), 136 (135), 147 (146), 148.
- Daniel 3: 35-68. 'Bless the Lord, all works of the Lord...'

- Matthew: 6: 25-34. 'Consider the lilies of the field...'
- Romans 8: 18-25. 'We know that the whole creation has been groaning in travail together until now.'

Friendship
- Ecclesiasticus (Sirach) 6: 5-17; '...the person that has found one [a friend] has found a treasure....'
- Matthew 11: 1-15. '...among those born of woman...no greater than John the Baptist...'
- John 11: 1-44. Lazarus raised from death; '...he whom you love is ill... Jesus wept...deeply moved.'
- John 20: 1-18. Mary Magdalene consoled by the appearance of Jesus.
- Luke 10: 38-42. Jesus' deep friendship with Martha and Mary (cf. John 11).

Formation
- Ephesians 4: 7-16. Attaining 'to the measure of the stature of the fullness of Christ.'
- Luke 2: 22-40. 'And the child grew and became strong...'
- Luke 2: 41-52. 'And Jesus increased in wisdom and in stature...'

God
- Matthew 1:23. Through Christ and the Church (Christian community), God is present in the world.
- Matthew 3: 1-17. 'It wasn't that a dove descended, because it doesn't say that a dove descended but "*like* a dove." It was the love of God that descended on him.' (Sally and Philip Scharper, eds., *The Gospel in Art by the Peasants of Solentiname*, New York: Orbis Books, 1984, p.22).
- Matthew 6: 7-15. 'It is a loving name [i.e. *Abba*] that's given to God...we don't have to be formal when we chat with God and give the name "papa".' (Sally and Philip Scharper, eds., The Gospel in Art , p.32).
- Matthew 6: 28-34. Abandonment - put ourselves in God's hands.
- Matthew 7: 1-5. God would not have us judge.
- Matthew 18: 21-35. The parable of the Unforgiving Servant - our God is forgiving (cf. also Luke 17: 3-4).
- Matthew 20: 1-16. The Workers in the Vineyard - God's justice much more ample than our notions of justice.
- Luke 10: 25-37. The Good Samaritan; Luke 15: 1-7, The Lost Sheep; Luke 15: 8-10, The Lost Coin. These passages testify to God's unconditional love, compassion, patience - loves to the point of foolishness (old man running) - patiently gives the barren fig tree another chance when all others would have given up on it - God a loving parent, not a scorekeeper.
- 1 John 4: 7-21; '...for God is love.'

God, presence of (and Holy Spirit)
- Matthew 1:23. Emmanuel - God with us.
- John 14: 8-14. The person who sees Jesus sees God.
- Acts 15: 22-29. 'For it has seemed good to the Holy Spirit and to us...'

God, will of
- Matthew 26: 36-46. '...not as I will, but as thou wilt.'

- John 4: 31-37. 'My food is to do the will of the one who sent me...'

Jesus
- Matthew 3: 13-15. Baptism of Jesus - '...we shall *do* all that God requires.'
- Matthew 4: 1-11. Temptations - Jesus *does* the will of God.
- Matthew 5: 21-48. Jesus calls for *more* - the kingdom demands it.
- Matthew 7: 15-20. Jesus a *doer* - a person for others.
- Matthew 8: 5-13. For Jesus faith (trust) indispensable.
- Matthew 9: 18-38. Jesus a *healer* - a person for others.
- Matthew 11: 1-6. Jesus makes an *option with the poor* - kingdom breaks in.
- Matthew 11: 25-30. Jesus knows the Father - yoke of Jesus may appear heavy, but in reality light.
- Matthew 12: 15-21. The *mercy* of Jesus - he 'does not break off the broken reed.'
- Matthew 16: 21-35 (cf. also Mark 8: 31- 9:1; Luke 9: 22-27). Prophecies of the Passion - *suffering* is part of the deal for those who follow Jesus.
- Matthew 18: 21-35. Parable of the Unforgiving Servant - Jesus is *forgiving*.
- Matthew 24: 29-31. Christ will come again.
- Matthew 25: 1-13. The Parable of the Ten Virgins - we must be *ready* for the coming of Jesus.
- Matthew 25: 31-46. '...for I was hungry and you gave me food, I was thirsty and you gave me drink...' This is one of the most eloquent pleas for justice in the Bible.
- Matthew 26:14 - 27:66 (shorter form, 27:11-54). The Passion.
- Mark 14:1 - 15:47 (shorter form, 15: 1-39).The Passion.
- Luke 22:14 - 23:56. (shorter form 23: 1-49). The Passion.
- John 18:1 - 19:42. The Passion.

Justice
- Exodus 3: 1-20. God the liberator.
- Exodus 6: 2-13. God the liberator.
- Exodus 22: 20-24. 'You shall not wrong or oppress the stranger....You shall not afflict any widow or orphan.'
- Deuteronomy 10: 16-20. 'He expects justice for the fatherless and widow, and loves the sojourner...'
- 1 Kings 21: 1-16. A grave injustice. (What are the injustices in your own area?)
- Isaiah 3: 13-15. Injustice condemned.
- Isaiah 58: 1-12. A change of heart, not just empty worship, is called for.
- Amos 2: 6-8. '...they that trample the head of the poor...'
- Amos 5: 21-24. 'Let justice roll down like waters...'
- Amos 6: 1-7. 'Woe to those who are at ease in Zion...'
- Amos 8: 4-7. 'Hear you who trample the needy...'
- Micah 6:8. 'Do justice, love kindness, walk humbly with our God.'
- Matthew 5: 27-30. Good must triumph over evil.
- Matthew 5: 38-42. Good must triumph over evil.
- Matthew 25: 31-40. 'I was hungry and you gave me food...'

- Luke 4: 16-21. Jesus' mission - option with the poor.
- Galatians 3: 26-29. Away with all barriers.

Kingdom
- Matthew 5: 3-12. The values of the kingdom - turn worldly values on their heads.
- Matthew 5-7. Requirements of the kingdom.
- Matthew 10. The messengers of the kingdom.
- Matthew 13. Parables of the kingdom; mysteries of the kingdom.
- Matthew 18: 21-35. The position of little children in the kingdom.
- Matthew 18: 21-35. Forgiveness, reconciliation.
- Matthew 24-25. Those who work for the kingdom must be watchful and faithful.
- 1 Corinthians 15: 12-28. There is tension - the kingdom is here, and yet to come.
- Galatians 6: 11-18. The kingdom is 'a new creation.'

Leadership/Coordination/Animation/Facilitation
- Matthew 20: 20-28. Authority is for service (cf. Mark 10: 35-45; Luke 22: 24-27).
- Luke 10: 1-2. Teamwork.
- Luke 22: 24-27. Be a servant.
- John 13: 1-20. Jesus washes his disciples feet.
- Galatians 2: 11-21. 'But when Cephas came to Antioch I opposed him to his face.'

Love (cf. Community)
- Mark 4: 35-41. Jesus calming the storm, 'lack of love in the world, that's the stormy lake.' (Sally and Philip Scharper, eds. *The Gospel in Art by the Peasants of Solentiname*, Maryknoll, New York: Orbis Books, 1984, p. 28).
- Luke 9: 10-17. The Multiplication of the Loaves: '...The gospel doesn't mention multiplication or miracle. It just says they shared...' (Sally and Philip Scharper, eds., *The Gospel in Art*, p.42).
- John 13:35. '...all will know that you are my disciples if you have love for one another.'
- 1 Corinthians 13. ' If you speak in the tongues of men and angels, but have not love...'
- 1 John 4: 7-21. God is love - love of neighbour - love drives out fear.

Option with the poor/ Mission (cf. Jesus)
- Matthew 10: 5-15 (cf. Mark 6: 7-13; Luke 9: 1-6). The mission of the twelve.
- Matthew 21: 12-17 (cf. Mark 11: 15-19; Luke 19: 45-48; John 2: 13-22). The clearing of the temple - we must not dare use religion or a holy place as a hideaway - 'den of robbers.'
- Mark 10:17-31; '...sell what you have, and give to the poor...'
- Luke 4: 16-21. Jesus is rejected at Nazareth - Jesus' mission: an option with the poor.
- Luke 10: 1-20. The mission of the seventy-two.

- 16: 19-31. The rich man and Lazarus - scraps from the rich man's table totally inadequate.
- Luke 18: 18-30. Jesus against possessiveness.
- Acts 11: 19-30. Mission to Antioch where the term *Christian* originated.
- 1 Thessalonians 4: 9-12. Christians to be witnesses.

Peace
- Leviticus 26: 3-13. The elements of peace.
- Judges 6: 19-24. Peace the gift of God.
- Psalm 35:27. God desires peace for us.
- Isaiah 2: 1-5. Turn swords into ploughshares.
- Isaiah 9: 5-7. Messiah the Prince of Peace - peace without and within the kingdom.
- Isaiah 32: 16-17. Justice the basis of peace.
- Isaiah 48: 17-19. Peace the fruit of obedience to God.
- Isaiah 48: 20-22. No peace for the wicked.
- Isaiah 54: 13-17. If Israel is just,· there will be peace and prosperity.
- Isaiah 60: 17-22. There will be peace and righteousness.
- Jeremiah 6: 13-15. Peace the fruit of justice, not of a lie.
- Ezekiel 13: 10-12. Saying there is peace when there is none is to white-wash a crumbling wall.
- Matthew 10: 11-13. A greeting of peace, once uttered, has a power of its own (cf. Luke 10: 5-6).
- Matthew 26: 51-53. Non-violence (cf. Luke 22: 49-53).
- John 14: 25-27. Peace of Jesus the only true peace (cf. John 16:33).
- Romans 8: 6-8. To enjoy peace one needs to be spiritually minded.
- Romans 14: 13-19. Peace is right relationships (harmony).
- 1 Corinthians 7: 12-16. God has called us to peace.
- 1 Corinthians 14: 26-33. Peace is right relationships (harmony).
- Ephesians 2: 14-17. Peace is union with God - Jesus our peace - unites us with God.
- Ephesians 6: 10-20. Preaching the gospel brings peace.
- Philippians 4: 4-7. Peace of God communicated through Jesus passes all understanding.
- Colossians 3: 14-15. We are called to peace because we are one - the body of Christ.

Planning and Evaluation
- Luke 10: 1-20. Christ prepares the apostles for their mission.
- Acts 6: 1- 7. The apostles evaluate a situation and plan.
- Acts 15: 1-35. The apostles evaluate a situation and plan.

Prayer
- Matthew 6: 5-15. How to pray.
- Romans 8: 26-27; '...the Spirit pleads with God for us...'
- Luke 6: 12-16; '...all night he continued in prayer to God.'
- Luke 8: 1-8. Pray without losing heart.

Prayer/Action (cf. Jesus - Doing - Doer)
- Matthew 7:21. 'Not everyone who says to me, 'Lord, Lord,' shall enter the kingdom...the person who *does* the will of my Father...'
- John 1: 1-14. The Word became *flesh.*
- Isaiah 29: 13-14. Lip service not enough.
- James 1: 22-25. 'but be doers of the word, and not hearers only...'
- James 2: 14-26. 'So faith by itself, if it has no works is dead.'

Process
- Ecclesiastes 3: 1-19. A time for everything.
- Mark 4: 1-8. 'The plants sprouted, grew, and produced corn...'
- Mark 4: 26-34. Seeds slowly growing - The Parable of the Mustard Seed (cf. Matthew 13: 31-32; Luke 13: 18-19).
- Luke 2:52. 'And Jesus increased in wisdom and stature...'
- Ephesians 4: 1-16. Attaining 'to the measure of the stature of the fullness of Christ.'

Readiness
- Luke 10:13; 10: 23-24; 11:29; 12: 16-21; 12:35; 12: 43-46; 12: 54-56; 12:57; 13: 1-5; 13: 6-9; 14:16; 14:28; 16:1-8; 17: 26-30; 19:5; 19:11-27 (cf. Matthew 35: 14-30).

Reconciliation
- Proverbs 24: 15-16; '...a righteous person falls seven times, and rises again...'
- Luke 3: 1-6. 'Prepare the way of the Lord...'
- Luke 7: 36-50. The woman who was a sinner anoints Jesus; 'her sins are forgiven...for she loved much.'
- Luke 17: 1-4. 'And if the same person sins against you seven times a day...you must forgive.'
- John 8: 1-11. The woman taken in adultery.
- 2 Corinthians 12: 5-10. Strength in weakness.

Women
- Genesis 1. God created human beings in the image and likeness of God - male and female God created them.
- Joshua 2: 1-24. Rahab astutely saves her family.
- Judges 4: 4-23. Deborah saviour and leader of her people.
- Ruth 1-4. Valiant women.
- 1 Samuel 9:11. Michal, Saul's daughter and David's wife, saves David.
- 1 Samuel 25: 14 - 42. The discreet Abigail prevents David from wrongfully shedding blood and saves lives.
- 2 Samuel 21: 7-14. The devotion of Rizpah.
- 2 Kings 4: 8-37. The woman of Shunem - wisdom and devotion.
- Judith 13: 1-20. Judith saves her people.
- Esther 7: 1-10. Esther saves her people.
- Matthew 15: 21-28. Jesus heals the woman of Syria (cf. Mark 7: 24-30).
- Matthew 25: 1-13. Jesus appreciates the concerns of women.
- Matthew 26: 6-13. Jesus anointed by a woman at Bethany - defends her against her critics.

- Mark 1: 29-31. Jesus cures Peter's mother-in-law (cf. Matthew 8: 14-17; Luke 4: 38-41).
- Mark 5: 21-43. Jesus raises the daughter of Jairus and heals the woman with the haemorrhage (cf. Matthew 9: 18-26; Luke 8: 40-56).
- Luke 7: 11-17. Jesus takes pity on the widow of Naim.
- Luke 8: 1-13. Women listed with the men as helpers of Jesus - various women later witnessed his death and resurrection.
- Luke 10: 38-42. Jesus' deep friendship with Martha and Mary (cf. John 11).
- Luke 13: 10-17. Jesus heals woman with the deformed back.
- Luke 15: 8-10. The Lost Coin. Jesus appreciates the concerns of women.
- Luke 18: 1-8. The Parable of the Widow and the Judge.
- John 4: 1-42. Jesus' respect for, and frankness with, the Samaritan woman - Jesus sends the apostles on mission two by two, but the Samaritan woman alone converts a whole village - Jesus' conduct towards women revolutionary.
- Acts 1: 12-14. Women important in the Church from the outset.
- Acts 12:12. Key role of women in the early Church.
- Acts 16: 11-15. Lydia readily hears the word of God.
- Acts 18: 24-28. Priscilla and Aquila equal partners in mission.
- Galatians 3: 26-29. Clearest statement of equality of the sexes in the New Testament.

Youth
- Exodus 2: 11-15. The young Moses.
- 1 Samuel, chapters 16, 17, 18. The young David.
- Tobit (Tobias) chapters 1-14. Much to say to modern youth.
- Proverbs 1: 8-9; 6:23; 10:1; 15:32; 17:25; 23:25; 27:17. Youth and the family.
- Canticle of Canticles (Song of Solomon), chapters 1-8. A song of human love.
- Jeremiah 1. The young Jeremiah.
- Daniel 13. The story of Susanna (or book of Susanna).
- Ecclesiasticus (Sirach), Youth and the School: 1: 22-24 (patience); 3: 17:20 (humility); 3: 21-23 (study of the law enough for the wise person); 3: 25-29 (invitation to meditate); 4: 20-31 (critical awareness); 5: 9-13 (firm in resolution, careful in speaking); 6: 2-4 (dominating one's passion); 7: 4-7 (no need to be ambitious); 7: 11, 32 (being compassionate); 18:30 - 19:3 (controlling one's desires); 20:27 (don't be easily influenced); 22: 16-18 (reflecting well before a decision); 23:7, 12-14 (wisdom in silence); 33: 4-6 (be wise and consistent); 37:7-15 (value of God's counsel); 37: 16-18 (communication through silence); 38:24 - 39:11 (eulogy of the teacher); 41:14 - 42:8 (a middle way between false modesty and brashness).
- Matthew 9: 20. Jesus appreciates youthful frankness.
- Mark 5: 35-43. Jesus helps the young girl.
- Mark 10: 13-16. '...whoever does not receive the kingdom of God like a child.'
- Mark 14: 51-52. Curiosity of the young man in Gethesemane.

- Luke 2: 41-52. The young Jesus provokes wonder.
- Luke 15: 11-32. Prodigal Son - harrowing experience, conversion.

Christian Family and Community, caring for:
- Ephesians 5:22 - 6:9; 6: 1-4.
- Colossians 3:18- 4:1.
- 1 Timothy 2:15; 3:4; 4:12; 5:4, 10.
- 2 Timothy 3:15.
- Titus 1: 5-6; 2: 6-8.
- Hebrews 12:7, 10.
- 1 Peter 2:13 - 3:7.
- 1 John 2: 13-14.

Notes

NOTES ON CHAPTER 1

1. Raymond E. Brown, *The Churches the Apostles Left Behind*, New York, Paulist Press, 1984, p.11.
2. Eduardo Hoornaert, *The Memory of the Christian People*, New York: Orbis Books, 1988, p. 198.
3. Michelle Connolly, Lecture, Paulian Centre, Sydney, Saturday, November 14th, 1992.
4. Bill Loader, *Colloquium*, 24/1 (1992), p. 8.
5. Leonardo Boff, *Ecclesiogenesis: The Base Communities Reinvent the Church*, Maryknoll, New York: Orbis Books, 1986, p.6.
6. Joseph G. Healey, *AFER*, Eldoret, Kenya: GABA Publications, vol. 30, no. 2, p. 76, April 1988.
7. Evelyn Eaton Whitehead and James D. Whitehead, *Community of Faith, Crafting Christian Communities Today*, Mystic, Connecticut: Twenty-Third Publications, 1992, p.19.
8. *National Catholic Reporter*, Kansas City, August 27, 1993, p.2.
9. Ibid, July 14, 1995, p.6.
10. *Seeking Gospel Justice in Africa*, Eldoret, Kenya: Gaba Publications, 1981.
11. *AFER, Centenary of the Evangelization in Kenya*, Eldoret, Kenya: Gaba Publications, vol. 32, no. 4, August 1990, pp. 186-191.
12. *The African Synod*, Kenya: Daughters of St. Paul, 1994.
13. *Tablet :* London, April 23rd., 1994, p.500.
14. AMECEA Documentation Service, Nairobi, Jan. 28, 1985, p.1.
15. Raymond Fung, *Household of God on China's Soil*, New York: Orbis Books, 1983.
16. Joseph Prased Pinto OFM Cap., *Inculturation Through Basic Communities*, Bangalore: Asian Trading Corporation, 1985, p. 176.
17. Ibid, p.176.
18. Peter Nemeshegyi, *Concilium*, London: SCM; New York: Orbis Books, volume 2, 1993, p. 119.
19. John O'Brien CSSp. *Seeds of a New Church*. Dublin: The Columba Press, 1994.
20. cf. *Tablet*, August 9th, 1980.

NOTES ON CHAPTER 2

1. Evelyn Eaton Whitehead & James D.Whitehead, *Community of Faith*, Mystic: cf. pp. 140-147.
2. Austin Flannery, *Vatican Council II, Evangelica Testificatio: Witness to the Gospel*, New York: Costello Publishing Company, no. 25, p. 692., Fifth Printing, 1980.
3. Jeanne Hinton, *Communities*, Eagle: Guildford, 1993, p.39.
4. Paul VI, *Populorum Progressio (Fostering the Development of Peoples)*, London: Catholic Truth Society, 1968, no. 81, p. 38.
5. Segundo Galilea, *The Future of Our Past*, Notre Dame, Indiana: Ave Maria Press, 1985, p.27.
6. Thomas Merton, *The Non-violent Alternative*, New York: Farrar, Strauss, Giroux, 1980, p. 64.

NOTES ON CHAPTER 4

1. Paul VI, *Populorum Progressio (Fostering the Development of Peoples)*, no. 32, p.17.
2. Dr Hill, *Cook Book*, London, 1747.

NOTES ON CHAPTER 5

1. Justice and Peace Commission of the Kenyan Bishops' Conference, *We are the Church: Lenten Campaign 1994*, Nairobi: St Joseph's Press, Kangemi, 1994, p.10.
2. *National Catholic Reporter*, October 27th, 1995, p. 2.
3. Justice and Peace Commission of the Kenyan Bishops' Conference, *We are the Church: Lenten Campaign 1994*, Nairobi: St Joseph's Press, Kangemi, 1994, p. 3.

NOTES ON CHAPTER 6

1. Dom Helder Camara, *Hoping Against All Hope*, Maryknoll, New York: Orbis Books, 1964, p. 189.

NOTES ON CHAPTER 7

1. Hugh O'Donnell, *Mrs Moody's Blues See Red*, Limerick: Salesian Press, 1980, p.10.
2. Evelyn Eaton Whitehead & James D. Whitehead, *Community of Faith, Crafting Christian Communities Today*, pp. 77-79.
3. Langdon Gilkey, *Message and Existence*, Minneapolis: Seabury Press, 1979, p. 165.
4. Ralph Hodgson, *Poems*, London: Macmillan, c. 1917.
5. Penny Lernoux, *The Cry of the People*, New York: Doubleday and Company, 1980, p. 267.
6. David J. O'Brien and Thomas Shannon (eds.) 'Justice in the World,' in *Renewing the Earth*, New York: Image Books, 1977, p. 391.

NOTES ON CHAPTER 8

1. Carlos Mesters, *The Bible and Liberation*, ed. Norman K. Gottwald, Maryknoll, New York: Orbis Books, 1983, p. 122.
2. Ibid.
3. Sally and Philip Scharper (eds), *The Gospel in Art by the Peasants of Solentiname*, Maryknoll, New York: Orbis Books, 1984, p.32.
4. Charles De Foucauld, *Oeuvres spirituelles (Antologie)*, Paris: Seuil, 1958, p.166.
5. *Oeuvres*, St Francis de Sales, eds, Andre Ravier and Roger Devos, Paris: Bibliotheque de la Pleiade, Editions Gallimard, 1969, III, 260.

NOTES ON THE CONCLUSION

1. Roberta Imboden, *From the Cross to the Kingdom*. San Francisco: Harper & Row, 1987, pp. 41-63.
2. Ibid, pp. 10-40.

Annotated Bibliography

Andrews, Dave with Engwicht, David. *Can You Hear the Heartbeat?* Sydney: Hodder and Stoughton, 1989. Describes the radical alternative to a me-first lifestyle in which the strong get power and the weak go to the wall.

Azevado, Marcelo, de C., SJ *Basic Ecclesial Communities in Brazil.* Washington, D.C.: Georgetown University Press, 1987. A thorough investigation of the "fascinating reality of Brazilian Basic Ecclesial Communities." The book is geared to the academic.

Banks, Robert and Julia. *The Church Comes Home: A New Base for Community and Mission.* Australia, Sutherland, NSW: Albatross Books, 1989; Oxford: Lion Publishing, 1989. Drawing on their own twenty-year experience of home Church, Robert and Julia Banks discuss life in a home Church in a very readable down-to-earth style. Gives a biblical, theological, and historical foundation for home Churches as well as practical advice on starting and maintaining them. An excellent read.

Banks, Robert. *Going to Church in the First Century.* Blacktown, NSW: Hexagon Press, 1985. An historically accurate fictionalization of one pagan's encounter with a first-century house Church. Helps peel away our cultural misconceptions of Church by seeing what things were like in the early Church. Interesting and provocative.

_____ *Paul's Idea of Community: the Early House Churches in their Historical Setting.* Grand Rapids, MI: Eerdman's Publishing, 1980. A fantastic rereading of the New Testament which will change your view of Church! Scholarly in tone yet easy to read, this book lays a solid biblical and theological foundation for Church as community.

Baranowski, Arthur R. *Creating Small Faith Communities.* Cincinnati, Ohio: St Anthony's Messenger Press, 1988. A methodology for establishing small Christian communities in parishes, written by one who has had considerable experience in the field.

Barret, Lois. *Building the House Church.* Scottdale, PA: Herald Press, 1986. A valuable guide to starting home Churches by an experienced leader of a network of home Churches in Wichita, Kansas. Deals with questions such as written covenants, worship, relationships, decision-making, growth strategies, and so on. The book's only flaw is an over-emphasis on structure and order.

Barriero, Alvaro, SJ *Basic Ecclesial Communities - The Evangelization of the Poor*. Maryknoll, New York: Orbis Books, 1982. This simply written book shows the power of the poor for evangelization, particularly when this power is harnessed in basic ecclesial communities.

Biagi, Bob. *A Manual for Helping Groups to Work More Effectively*. University of Massachusetts, Amherst, MA. A book that reads easily and may be adapted for use by small Christian communities; it has useful suggestions for group dynamics or exercises.

Boadt, Lawrence. *Reading the Old Testament: An Introduction*. New York: Paulist Press, 1984. Used by students in the early years of university or late years of secondary (high) school.

Boff, Leonardo. *Ecclesiogenesis: The Base Communities Reinvent the Church*. Maryknoll, New York: Orbis Books, 1986. The author explains how the Brazilian basic Christian communities are a new way of being Church.

_____ *Jesus Christ, Liberator*. Maryknoll, New York: Orbis Books, 1978. Refreshing insights on Jesus.

Brown, Raymond E. *The Churches the Apostles Left Behind*. Mahwah, New Jersey: Paulist Press, 1984. In New Testament times the Church was not a monolith - there were various models operating.

Byrne, Tony, CSSp. *Working for Justice and Peace: A Practical Guide*. Ndola, Zambia: Mission Press, 1988. A practical and easy to read guidebook for people who wish to encourage and motivate themselves and others to take action for justice and peace. Byrne is very experienced in the field.

_____ *How to Evaluate*. Ndola, Zambia: Mission Press, 1988. A practical guide to evaluate the work of the Church and its organizations.

Center for Conflict Resolution. *Building United Judgments: a Handbook for Consensus Decision Making*. Madison, WI., 1981. Although not a "Christian" book in itself, this is an invaluable how-to guide to the form of decision-making most appropriate for Christian community: consensus. Extremely practical and thorough. Highly recommended.

Concilium, London: SCM; New York: Orbis Books, vol. 2, 1993. A most enlightening number regarding the Church in Asia.

Cook, Guillermo. *The Expectation of the Poor - Latin American Basic Ecclesial Communities in Protestant Perspective*. Maryknoll, New York: Orbis Books, 1985. The most complete treatment of this theme, adapted from a doctoral thesis.

Crosby, Michael H. *House of Disciples - Church, Economics and Justice*. Maryknoll, New York: Orbis Books, 1988. Through an in-depth exploration of Matthew's Gospel and its socioeconomic milieu, this book shows how the world of the early Church continues to challenge Christians today. It makes a unique contribution to both New Testament scholarship and the practice of contemporary spirituality.

Cruden, Alexander, M.A. *Concordance of the Holy Scriptures*. London: The Epworth Press, 1969. Most useful in helping resource persons to locate scripture passages.

Culling, Elizabeth. *What is Celtic Spirituality?* Nottingham: Grove Books Limited, 1993. In this book we find brief, clear, quality thinking that addresses its subject capably.

Dearling, Alan, and Armstrong, Howard. *The Youth Games Book.* I.T. Resource Centre, Quarries Homes, Bridge of Weird, Renfrewshire, Scotland, 1980. Useful exercises for youth.

de la Torre, Ed., *Touching Ground Taking Root.* Quezon City (Philippines): Socio-Pastoral Institute, 1986. This book gives an account of small Christian communities in the Philippines.

de Sales, Francis, Jane de Chantal. *Letters of Spiritual Direction.* New York, Paulist Press, 1988. A rich correspondence which reveals the joint spirituality of two great experts in the spiritual life. The Introduction, too, is really valuable.

Donders, Joseph G. *Empowering Hope: Thoughts to Brighten Your Day.* Mystic, Connecticut: Twenty-Third Publications, 1985. This simple down-to-earth book is a collection of inspirational radio and television presentations broadcast in many parts of the world; could provide excellent material for meetings.

Donovan, Vincent, CSSp. *Christianity Rediscovered.* Maryknoll, New York: Orbis Books, 1982. An account of a missionary endeavour among the Masai people in Tanzania which makes one think about the Church in a wonderfully creative way.

Dorr, Donal. *Option for the Poor: A Hundred Years of Vatican Social Teaching.* Maryknoll, New York: Orbis Books, 1983; Dublin: Gill and Macmillan, 1983. An excellent scholarly survey of the period under consideration.

Drane, John. *Introducing the Bible.* Oxford: Lion Publishing, 1990. A simple introduction. Exists only in hardback.

Dublin Diocesan Committee for Parish Development and Renewal. *Parish Development and Renewal.* Dublin: Veritas Publications, 1993. An account by the Committee of the attempts being made to animate parishes.

Dulles, Avery, SJ *Models of the Church.* Dublin: Gill and Macmillan, 1976; New York: Image Books, Doubleday and Company, 1978. This book shows us that the Church is not just one simple reality, but can express itself in various forms or models.

Eagleson, John, and Scharper, Philip (eds). *Puebla and Beyond.* Maryknoll, New York: Orbis Books, 1979. Included is the opening address of John Paul II to the Bishops' Conference in Puebla.

Earley, Ciaran, OMI (ed). *Parish Alive Alive O!* Dublin: The Columba Press, 1985. This is an account of efforts to establish small Christian communities in a variety (urban and rural) of Dublin parishes.

Edwards, Denis, and Wilkinson, Bob. *The Christian Community Connection: A Program for Small Christian Communities.* Adelaide, Australia: Community for the World Movement, 1992. This book introduces small communities to the changing world, changing Church.

Éla, Jean Marc. *African Cry.* Maryknoll, New York: Orbis Books, 1986. A profoundly prophetic voice from the African Church. Strong on issues of justice and inculturation.

Figueroa Deck, Allan; Tarango, Yolanda; and Matovina, Timothy M (eds). *Perspectives: New Insights into Hispanic Ministry.* Kansas City: Sheed and Ward, 1995. A work that probes the tensions, issues, and options facing the Church as Hispanic ministry continues to develop and deepen in the United States.

Flannery, Austin (ed.). *Vatican II: Conciliar and Post-Conciliar Documents.* Dublin: Dominican Publications, 1975; New York: Costello Publishing Co., 1975.

_____ *More Post-Conciliar Documents,* Dublin: Dominican Publications, 1982; New York: Costello Publishing Company, 1982.

Fraser, Margaret and Ian. *Wind and Fire - The Spirit Reshapes the Church in Basic Christian Communities.* Basic Communities Resource Centre, S.C.C., Dunblane FK15 OAJ, Scotland, 1986.This book gives us the opportunity to feel the life of the small Christian communities. In it the communities speak for themselves.

Fraser, Ian. *Reinventing Theology as the People's Work.* Glasgow: Wild Goose Publications, 1988. Shows how theology is not just the project of the academic but of the entire Christian community.

_____ *Living a Countersign.* Glasgow: Wild Goose Publications, 1990. The enormously experienced author seeks to explain basic Christian communities in terms of their historical roots, their distinctive features, and their experiences of struggle.

_____ *Strange Fire: Life Stories and Prayers.* Glasgow: Wild Goose Publications, 1994. This work brings together 90 stories from Ian Fraser's many years among Christian communities around the world. Inspiring, well drawn, and always thought-provoking, they bring to life the profound faith of ordinary people, often in extremes of hardship and danger. Each finishes with a prayer or reflection which lets us link the stories with those of our own daily lives. The volume could prove an invaluable resource for meetings of the small Christian communities.

Fung, Raymond. *Household of God on China's Soil.* Maryknoll, New York: Orbis Books, 1983. A refreshing collection of first-hand experiences of fourteen Chinese Christian communities during the turbulent Cultural Revolution years.

Gaba Publications. *African Cities and Christian Communities.* Spearhead No. 72, Eldoret, Kenya, 1982. A good study by people with local knowledge.

Galilea, Segundo. *The Future of Our Past.* Notre Dame, Indiana: Ave Maria Press, 1985. One is struck by how relevant the spirituality of the great Spanish mystics is to modern times, and it is particularly suited to the small Christian communities.

Gish, Art. *Living in Christian Community.* Scottdale, PA: Herald Press, 1978. An excellent book on Christian community. Written from an Anabaptist perspective, it comprehensively addresses the important theological and organizational issues. Both solidly theoretical and extremely practical.

Gutierrez, Gustavo. *A Theology of Liberation*. Maryknoll, New York: Orbis Books, 1973. A most important book that created a watershed in theology.

Healey, Joseph G., MM *A Fifth Gospel - The Experience of Black Christian Values*. Maryknoll, New York: Orbis Books, 1981. Gives valuable insights into the workings of small Christian communities in Africa.

Healy, Sean, SMA and Brigid Reynolds. *Social Analysis in the Light of the Gospel*. Dublin: Folens and Co., 1983. A useful volume that emerged from a series of workshops.

Hebblethwaite, Margaret. *Basic is Beautiful*. London: Fount (HarperCollins Publishers), 1993. This volume deals with the issue of how to translate basic ecclesial communities from the Third World to the First. Includes valuable accounts of, and reflection on, practical experiences.

Hennelly, Alfred T., SJ, ed., *Santo Domingo and Beyond*. Maryknoll, New York: Orbis Books, 1993. Documents and commentaries from the historic meeting of the Latin American Bishops' Conference.

Hinton, Jeanne. *Communities*. Guildford (Surrey), Eagle: Inter Publishing Service, 1993. Gives the instructive stories and spiritualities of twelve European communities. The volume is enhanced with photographs by Christopher Phillips.

_____ *Walking in the Same Direction*. Geneva: WCC Publications, 1995. The author, who has considerable experience, examines the new Church that is emerging in the world largely through the vision and action of the small communities.

Hirmer, Oswald. *How to Start Neighbourhood Gospel Groups*. Lumko Missiological Institute, P. O. Box 5058, Delmenville 1483, South Africa. A kit with posters and textbook for learning a method of gospel sharing by a man very experienced in the field.

Hodgson, Ralph. *Poems*. London: Macmillan, c. 1917.

Holland, Joe and Henriot, Peter, SJ *Social Analysis: Linking Faith and Justice*. Maryknoll, New York: Orbis Books, 1983. A valuable book by two experienced practitioners. Suited for animators of groups.

Hoornaert, Eduardo. *The Memory of the Christian People*. Maryknoll, New York: Orbis Books, 1988. This excellent work reveals striking similarities between the Church's first communities and the grassroots communities transforming the Church today. It puts us in touch with useful documentation from the early Church, thereby providing a sound historic base.

Hope, Anne, and Timmel, Sally. *Training for Transformation; A Handbook for Community Workers*. 3 vols. Gweru, Zimbabwe: Mambo Press, 1984. These volumes are excellent for justice formation and provide useful group exercises or dynamics.

Huelsmann, Fr, SJ *Pray - An Introduction to the Spiritual Life for Busy People*. Mahwah, New Jersey: Paulist Press, 1976 (comes with a Moderator's Manual). A 'course' in prayer to be used alone or in groups. Some communities in the United States have found this book most helpful.

Imboden, Roberta. *From the Cross to the Kingdom*. San Francisco: Harper and Row, 1987. Basing herself on the philosophy of Sartre, the author says much that is of interest to small Christian communities; brilliant and original.

Jackson, Dave and Neta. *Living Together in a World Falling Apart*. Altamonte Springs, Florida: Creation House Publishers, 1974. This book sparked much interest in small Christian communities when first published. Years later it is still relevant. Deals with the most basic questions - from theology of community to issues of who does the housework - in a very readable way.

John Paul II. *Redemptor Hominis*. London: Catholic Truth Society, 1979.

_____ *Laborem Exercens (On Human Work)*. London: Catholic Truth Society, 1981.

_____ *This is the Laity* (Simplification of *Christifideles Laici*). England: The Grail, 1989.

Justice and Peace Commission of the Kenyan Bishops' Conference. *We are the Church*, Lenten Campaign '94. Nairobi: St. Joseph's Press, Kangemi, 1994.

Kalilombe, Patrick A. *From Outstation to small Christian Community*. Eldoret, Kenya: Gaba Publications, 1981. A study, adapted from a doctoral thesis, by a person who was himself one of the pioneers in fostering small Christian communities in Africa. Shows how having a small number of people doesn't necessarily constitute a small Christian community.

Latin American Bishops. *The Church in the Present-Day Transformation of Latin America in the Light of the Council* (Medellin documents). Washington D.C. (Secretariat for Latin America, National Conference of Bishops), 3rd ed., 1979.

Lee, Bernard J. and Cowan, Michael A. *Dangerous Memories*. Kansas City: Sheed and Ward, 1986. Explores home Churches in the United States. Includes valuable discussion of mutuality, political action, and servant leadership. Contains an especially useful treatment of the role and potential of communities in the context of American individualism.

Lernoux, Penny. *Cry of the People*. Middlesex: Penguin, 1981; New York: Doubleday, 1980. An excellent resource book regarding the justice issue in Latin America. Particularly good on the National Security State and the role of the multinationals.

Le Shan, Lawrence. *How to Meditate*. Boston: Bantam Books, Little Brown and Company, 1974. A book that many people have found helpful.

Lobinger, Fritz. *Building Small Christian Communities*. Lumko Missiological Institute, P.O. Box 5058, Delmenville 1483, South Africa, 1981. A kit with large posters and textbook for starting small Christian communities; widely used, especially in Africa.

McCarthy, Flor, SDB *Windows on the Gospel: Stories and Reflections*. Dublin: Dominican Publications; Mystic, Connecticut: Twenty-Third Publications, 1992. This simple collection of stories and reflections is offered to all who are searching for a spirituality based on the gospel; excellent material for meetings.

McConnell, Frank. *Find Quickly in the Gospels*, Sevenoaks (Kent): Petrus Books, 1990. An extremely user-friendly guide for locating gospel texts - an ordinary person's concordance.

McDonagh, Sean. *The Greening of the Church*. Maryknoll, New York: Orbis Books, 1990. Effectively highlights the crucial environmental issue, theologically and practically.

Marins, José. *Church from the Roots*. London: CAFOD, 1989. Proceeding from modern-day parables, the author and his team, who have shared worldwide on small Christian communities, draw valuable conclusions for the groups.

Mesters, Carlos. *Defenceless Flower*. Maryknoll, New York: Orbis Books, 1989. Shows a marvellous use of the Bible in Brazilian small Christian communities.

Miller, Hal. *Christian Community: Biblical or Optional?* Ann Arbor: Servant Books, 1979. A solid theology of Christian community, demonstrating from the scriptures that community was part of God's plan from the beginning and that Jesus restored community through the kingdom.

NACCAN (National Association of Christian Communities and Networks, Britain). *Directory of Christian Communities and Networks*. Washington: JAS Print, 1993.

National Secretariat and Hispanic Teams. *Basic Ecclesial Communities*. Missouri 63057: Ligouri, 1980. Simple, theologically rich, and practical.

_____ *Guidelines for Establishing Basic Christian Communities in the United States*. Missouri 63057: Ligouri, 1981.

O'Brien, David J. and Shannon, Thomas A. *Renewing the Earth*. New York: Image Books, 1977. The single most comprehensive available collection of primary documents on Catholic social thought from Pope Leo XIII's *Rerum Novarum* (1891) to John Paul II's *Centesimus Annus* (1991). Documents are accompanied by introductory essays and helpful notes.

O'Brien, John, CSSp. *Seeds of a New Church*, Dublin: Columba Press, 1994. This deals with twenty-two group experiences in the Irish context and their implications for the Church of the future. Important and challenging reading particularly for anyone connected with the Church in Ireland.

Ó Donnchadha, Proinsias. *A Stack of Stories*. Dublin: Night Owl Early Bird Bureau, 1995. Beautiful short reflections that could provide valuable materials for meetings.

O'Donnell, Hugh, *Mrs Moody's Blues See Red*, Limerick: Salesian Press, 1980.

O'Gorman, Frances Elsie. *Base Communities in Brazil: Dynamics of a Journey*. Rio de Janeiro: FASE-NUCLAR, 1983. An account of Brazilian small Christian communities by one who has been deeply involved with them in the *favelas* of Rio de Janeiro.

O'Halloran, James. *Signs of Hope: Developing Small Christian Communities*, Maryknoll, New York: Orbis Books, 1991; Dublin: Columba Press, 1991. This book developed from *Living Cells* 'which has been for some years one of the best introductions to the small Christian communities' (*Tablet*, 22 February 1992). The current work, *Small Christian*

Communities, builds on both. *Signs of Hope* gives experiences of small Christian communities with which the author was personally involved.

_____ *The Least of These*. Dublin (Columba Press), 1991. A book of short stories, some of which have been used in catechetical programmes and courses on peace and justice.

O'Hanlon, Joseph. *Beginning the Bible*. Slough (England): St Paul's, 1994. A user-friendly, integrated introduction to the Bible. The general reader will find this amenable.

O'Regan, Pauline, and O'Connor, Teresa. *Community, Give it a Go!* Christchurch, New Zealand: Allen and Unwin, 1989. The authors describe their work in building community: how to establish networks, how to start a coffee group, ways of arranging childcare, kinds of celebrations, relationships between local community workers and professional groups.

Paul VI. *Populorum Progressio* (*On the Development of Peoples*). London: CTS, 1967; Mahwah, New Jersey: Paulist Press, 1967.

_____ *Evangelii Nuntiandi* (*Evangelization Today*). Dublin: Dominican Publications, 1977. Commentary by Bede McGregor O.P.

_____ *Evangelica Testificatio: Witness to the Gospel* (cf. above, Flannery. *Vatican Council II*, p. 680ff.)

_____ *Octogesima Adveniens* (*On Social Justice*). London: CTS, 1971

Perkins, Pheme. *Reading the New Testament, An Introduction*. New York: Paulist Press, 1977. Students in the latter years of secondary or high school or the early years of college or university will find this introduction useful.

Prased Pinto, Joseph, OFM Cap. *Inculturation through Basic Communities: An Indian Perspective*. Bangalore: Asia Trading Company, 1985. The author explores the potential of basic communities to create a Church that will be deeply rooted in the Indian values of religiosity, poverty, joy, and festivity.

Rahner, Karl, SJ *I Remember*. London: SCM, 1984. An autobiographical account, taken from an interview, of one who has been described as the 'quiet mover' and 'ghostwriter' of Vatican II, and even as 'the Father of the Church in the 20th Century.' The volume gives his thinking on the Council.

Raines, John C. and Day-Lower, Donna C. *Modern Work and Human Meaning*. Philadelphia, Pennsylvania: Westminster Press, 1986. This work deals with social problems in the United States. It has the considerable merit of allowing the poor to speak for themselves; listening to their voice is even more critical in the present political climate..

Reichert, Richard. *Simulation Games - for Religious Education*. Winona, Minnesota: St Mary's Press, Christian Brothers' Publications, 1975. Useful resource material.

Research and Development Division, National Council of Young Mens' Christian Associations, 291 Broadway, New York, 10007. *Training Volunteer Leaders - A Handbook to Train Volunteers and Other Leaders of Program Groups*. Contains helpful resource material and group exercises.

Scharper, Sally and Philip, eds. *The Gospel in Art by the Peasants of Solentiname*. Maryknoll, New York: Orbis Books, 1984. This book shows how the gospels can be used effectively by ordinary people.

SECAM. *Seeking Gospel Justice in Africa*. Eldoret, Kenya: Gaba Publications, 1981.

Snyder, Howard. *Community of the King*. Chicago: Inter-Varsity Press. 1977. On alternative Church models as agents of the kingdom. Very practical reading about Christian community based on an experience in the Irving Park Free Methodist Church in Chicago.

The African Synod. Kenya: Daughters of St Paul, 1994.

Torres, Sergio, Eagleson, John, eds. *The Challenge of Basic Christian Communities*. Maryknoll, New York: Orbis Books, 1981. Reflections on small Christian communities by some of the most eminent people in the fields of theology and pastoral practice from the South. Chapter 16 has information on the use of the Bible in small communities by Carlos Mesters, which is most enlightening.

Vanier, Jean. *Community and Growth* (Revised Edition). London: Darton, Longman and Todd, 1989. A veritable gold-mine of reflective and practical ideas on community by the founder of L'Arche.

Veritas. *Come and See: A New Vision of Parish Renewal*. Dublin: Veritas Publications, 1993. An account of a parish cell system pioneered in Ballinteer, Dublin.

Weber, Hans-Ruedi. *The Book that reads me*. Geneva: WCC Publications, 1995. A worthwhile handbook for Bible study enablers.

Whitehead, Evelyn Eaton and James D. *Community of Faith: Crafting Christian Communities Today*. Mystic, Connecticut: Twenty-Third Publications, 1992. An enormously valuable book which creatively employs the insights of modern psychology and sociology to help understand the nature and dynamics of Christian community. Strong as both a theoretical analysis of community and a practical guide to life in community.

Wiltgen, Ralph, SVD, *The Rhine Flows into the Tiber*. Devon, England: Augustine Publishing Company, 1978. This book highlights the German influence at Vatican II.

Index

Maritime Follow-up, 39-41
Minjung, (aware people) 29
Minjung Theology (Korea), 29
Mission
 to promote community model of Church, 26
 need to be in mission, 21
Momentum, means for maintaining in small Christian community, 118
Money, problems with, 27
Mothers of St Anne (Africa), 111
Motivation, 107, 114
Mozambique, 57
Muslims
 inter-faith dialogue with, 28
 part of religious heritage of Asia, 27
 working together with, 117
NACCAN, 188
Nairobi, 122 (Holy Family Basilica),
NAMMA (North American Maritime Ministry Association), 40
National Alliance of Parishes Restructuring into Communities (US), 21
National Catholic Reporter, (US), 7, 20, 22, 112, 179
National Pastoral Plan for Hispanic Ministry (US 1977), 22
National Secretariat and Hispanic Teams, 188
Nazareth, 16
NBCLC, Bangalore, publishes resource material for small Christian community, 29
Nemeshegyi, Peter, 30, 179
Neo-Catechumenate, 34
Network (linkage), 106-107
New England, Puritan community of the seventeenth century in, 20
New Mexico, 23
New Pentecost, 12
New Testament, small Christians communities in, 12-16
New Ways of Being Church (Birmingham, England, title of course), 36
New Zealand, small Christian communities in, 32-33
Newman Societies (Australia), 30
Nigeria, 67
North, the, 46, 79
North America (USA and Canada), historical profile of small Christian communities in, 19-23
North American Forum for Small Christian Communities (diocesan personnel), 21
Northern Ireland
 peace process in, 21/22, 38
 Corrymeela and reconciliation in, 67
Notre Dame University, and small Christian communities, 21
Oceania, 33